KF 1083 .T73 1999
OCLC: 40762770
Investing and managing
 trusts under the new

S0-AGT-681

DATE DUE	
MAR 23 2003	
Apr. 13	
APR - 8 2003	

GAYLORD

Investing and Managing Trusts under the New Prudent Investor Rule

Investing and Managing Trusts under the New Prudent Investor Rule

A Guide for Trustees, Investment Advisors, and Lawyers

John Train
and
Thomas A. Melfe

Harvard Business School Press
Boston, Massachusetts

THE RICHARD STOCKTON COLLEGE
OF NEW JERSEY LIBRARY
POMONA. NEW JERSEY 08240

Copyright 1999 John Train and Thomas A. Melfe

All rights reserved

Printed in the United States of America

03 02 01 00 99   5 4 3 2 1

Library of Congress Cataloging-in-Publication Data
Train, John.
    Investing and managing trusts under the new prudent investor rule
    a guide for trustees, investment advisors, and lawyers / John
Train, Thomas A. Melfe.
      p. cm.
    Includes index.
    ISBN 0-87584-861-3 (alk. paper)
    1. Legal investments—United States. 2. Trusts and trustees—United States.
3. Prudent person rule—United States. I. Melfe, Thomas A. II. Title.
KF1083.T73—1999
346.7305′9—dc21   99-18403
                                                   CIP

The paper used in this publication meets the requirements of the American National
Standard for Permanence of Paper for Printed Library Materials Z39.49-1984.

To Our Wives

Francie

and

Opal Lee

The basic underlying concern of the prudent investor standard is to shift the focus from whether a particular investment product is prudent to whether the overall investment process and strategy is designed to yield the desired results for the beneficiaries.

—THE SUPPORT MEMORANDUM FOR THE UNIFORM ACT

Contents

List of Figures and Tables

Acknowledgments

We are exceedingly grateful to Sara Perkins, for editoral coordination. Also to Ruth Ann Waite, Darlene Beauchamp, and Patricia Whitfield, for typing the manuscript, and to Kirsten Sandberg, for astute editing.

Introduction

The next few years will see the greatest transfer of wealth in our history. By the year 2010, over $10 trillion will pass from the present oldest generation to their families, a sum equal to the recent value of all the companies listed on the stock exchange. Much of this huge sum will be in the form of trusts. Internal Revenue Service data indicate that the number of trusts could increase by 50 percent over the next five years.

Few of us are familiar with how trusts operate, and still fewer with the rules that trustees must follow. We are taken by surprise when a parent or spouse dies, or grandparents create a trust for our children, and we are named trustee and thrust into responsibility. We soon discover that the office of trustee cannot be learned on the job. Investing has become so complicated that one can no longer be a trustee in name only, for the honor of it, or as a favor to a relative or friend. On the other hand, the job can be useful and rewarding if one is prepared.

This book, then, tells a trustee how to manage a trust in conformity with the many new Prudent Investor rules to which he must conform. (It is not, however, a basic how-to guide for inexperienced investors. For that, other books are available.)

Recently a central trust rule changed profoundly. Beginning in 1992 with the promulgation of a uniform model statute that has already been adopted by over half the states, the traditional Prudent Man Rule that governed trustees was replaced by a new Prudent Investor Rule. That is the reason for this book. We should soon have a uniform rule of prudent trust investing in all fifty states.

While we offer practical advice that trustees can use in the exercise of their investment authority under the New Rule, this book should also help the professionals who advise trustees on investing: investment managers, lawyers, stockbrokers, financial planners, trust departments, and family offices. And the revolutionary delegation of investment powers introduced by the New Rule should be a marketing opportunity for the investment industry.

Chapter 6 is devoted to issues of special interest to lawyers who have trustee clients or who counsel investment advisors. However, it is not intended as a dissertation or original legal research, nor should it be relied on as legal advice. Trustees and their advisors should seek advice from specialized counsel.

Trustees of private trusts are held to the highest standards of conduct known to our legal system. We hope this book will help its readers meet those standards.

As practitioners ourselves, we well appreciate that many investors, trustees, investment professionals, and lawyers are women. Nevertheless, we follow the old "he" convention, meaning it to be non-gender-specific, and less clumsy and pedantic than he/she.

We presume that many users of this book will want to consult specific sections from time to time. To permit that, we sometimes repeat ideas that also occur elsewhere. This is intentional. A nonprofessional will encounter unfamiliar terms; please consult the glossary.

Investing and Managing Trusts under the New Prudent Investor Rule

Trusts and Trustees

The Trust

Trusts are not only for the rich. They are used for amounts as small as $10,000. Because they are often a private family matter, few facts are available on their number or average size. Bankers' associations compile data for bank trust departments, but this information reflects only a small portion of all trusts, since most trustees are family members, not banks. As a guess, the average size of all currently active American trusts is probably between $50,000 and $100,000. (One must consider whether the trust form is practical when the amounts involved are small.)

Origin of the Trust

The trust dates back to William the Conqueror. It permitted the owner of land to control its disposition over extended periods, even after his death, while confiding the land's use or benefit, but not its legal owner-ship, to other persons during the term of the trust. As the years passed, the trust became used for property other than land, such as farm equip-ment, collectibles, livestock, art, and furniture. Eventually, almost anything an individual could own could be trusteed, although it was not until the early nineteenth century that trusts were allowed to hold stocks and bonds.

The trust concept was brought to North America by English colonists. Until the first half of the twentieth century, only very wealthy Americans could afford trusts. As individual American wealth expanded following World War II, and with the enactment of more complex tax laws, estate planners turned to the trust as an efficient instrument for the disposition of individual wealth. By the early 1960s a high percentage of prosperous Americans had embraced trusts for estate planning. The movement in that direction has never stopped.

The use of trusts today is confined primarily to the United States, Britain, and former British colonies. They are almost unknown elsewhere, although in recent years there has been a movement among international lawyers' groups to introduce trusts as a way of transferring multicountry estates.

A body of trust law has long governed how trusts may be used and how they are to be managed by trustees. In its early stages this law was very restrictive, primarily because a trust by its nature involves a fiduciary relationship, which means having a duty toward others. The law chose to impose on the fiduciary its highest standard of conduct. That remains true to this day.

Trusts Defined

The trust has survived the centuries relatively unchanged, because of its intrinsic power and versatility. It permits an owner to give varying interests in property to more than one person, over a designated period and for a variety of purposes that suit the owner's objectives, while giving a third party the responsibility of carrying out his wishes. This almost amounts to being able to write one's own law.

The two main categories of trusts are living trusts and testamentary trusts. A trust established during the life of its creator is a living or inter vivos trust, and the person who creates it is variously called the settlor, the trustor, or the grantor. When created by a will, it is known as a testamentary trust or a trust under will. The creator is the testator.

Living and testamentary trusts are almost identical. They differ mainly in grammatical style, with living trusts using the third person (e.g., "the income of the trust shall be paid to the settlor's issue") and testamentary trusts using the first person (e.g., "I direct that the income of the trust shall be paid to my issue"). Both trusts have income beneficiaries, a trustee or trustees, and a remainderman or remaindermen who take the property when the trust ends. Living trusts are funded as soon as the settlor adds property to them. A testamentary trust is activated only when the testator dies. Some trusts, both living and testamentary, are court supervised, meaning that under state law the trust and the trustee's activities are subject to court monitoring. Others are not, and they come under court power only when a trustee or beneficiary seeks the court's assistance. Which course is followed depends on state law. The trend is away from court supervision.

Parties to a Trust

A trust[1] is a legal relationship among four parties or, strictly speaking, categories of parties: a settlor, a trustee (or trustees), a life or term beneficiary (or beneficiaries), and the remainderman. Generally, anyone who is an adult under state law (usually age eighteen or older) can create a trust. The settlor transfers legal title in the property to the trustee of the trust as a fiduciary, while the beneficial interest in the property (income and capital) is assigned to persons designated by name or by class, as in the phrase "my issue." The beneficiaries are divided into two groups, known as the income beneficiaries, entitled to the income of the trust's investments, and the remaindermen, in whom title to the trust property vests when the trust terminates. The same person may be (but usually is not) both an income beneficiary and a remainderman, as with a trust for a minor who receives income until reaching his majority, when he receives the principal.

Trust Characteristics

A basic principle of trust law is that the terms of a trust will ordinarily govern the authority and duties of a trustee, to the extent that those terms are possible and legal. The terms can be restrictive, forbidding an otherwise

---

[1] By *trust* we mean both a living trust created by a settlor and a testamentary trust created by will. *Settlor* also means *testator*.

proper activity of the trustee, or they can expand his authority, permitting actions that may be generally considered improper for a trustee. In other words, the settlor of a trust has wide freedom to impose mandatory provisions and to bestow discretionary authority on a trustee. The terms of the trust, therefore, are extremely important for the trustee to understand and to follow diligently, since they control, except in the very limited cases where state law supersedes them; for example, a trust may not excuse a trustee from the duty to exercise care, skill, and caution, his fundamental obligation under trust law.

Trusts for individuals cannot last forever, although trusts for charities may. The length of time that a trust for an individual can last—its term—is governed by a legal principle known as the *rule against perpetuities,* which limits a trust term to the lives of a reasonable number of persons living and identified when the trust is created. An example of a trust term is: "This trust shall last until the death of the survivor of a class consisting of my spouse and my issue who are living on the date hereof." This phrase would be used in a living trust agreement. In a trust under a will, which becomes operative only upon the creator's death, the language would be modified to provide for the same class of persons, but, rather than specifying "on the date hereof" as the start of the trust term, it would read "until the death of the survivor of my wife and issue who survive me." The persons whose lives are used for the trust term are known as the measuring lives. The rule against perpetuities permits a period of twenty-one years beyond the last measuring life's death before a trust must end.

Qualifications of Trustees

State law governs the qualifications of trustees of private trusts. Most states allow anyone who is of age to serve. At least one trustee must reside in the state (or, if an institution, such as a bank, be authorized to do business there). There are a few exceptions, such as limitations on when non–U.S. citizens can serve. Convicted felons are usually disqualified. There is no upper age limit to acting as a trustee, nor any required investment experience or other specific skills.

Trust companies and banks with trust charters are authorized to serve as trustees. Certain organizations may not serve as private trustees, notably law and accounting firms, insurance companies (except one with a chartered trust subsidiary), business corporations, or other business or professional organizations, unless so authorized under state law. A partner or officer of these organizations can individually serve as a private trustee, however.

A trust fund typically consists of cash and securities, although occasionally it will hold a residence or other real estate. It has two interests: the principal and the income produced by that principal.

Income Beneficiaries

Income beneficiaries are of two types: mandatory, meaning that under the terms of the trust all income must be regularly paid out, and discretionary, leaving the decision to the trustee to pay or not pay out all trust income in any period. This is usually called a power to spray or power to sprinkle. Income not paid out is usually added to trust principal and reinvested.

The discretionary power to spray or sprinkle is usually left to the trustee, who might be governed by language such as "in such amounts and at such times, or not at all, and for any reason, to the exclusion of one or more persons if there is more than one in the class, as my trustees shall determine in their absolute discretion." Alternatively, the trust document can make the trustees' discretionary power over income subject to an objective standard (e.g., "as my trustees shall determine necessary and appropriate for the support and maintenance of the income beneficiary"). The full and unlimited discretion approach is the most common.

Some income beneficiaries also receive the power to withdraw trust principal from time to time or upon specified events, such as certain birthdays. However, the power to withdraw has potential adverse income tax results to the beneficiary, and for that reason is used sparingly by trust planners.

Principal Beneficiaries

There are also two types of principal beneficiaries: remaindermen and principal invasion discretionary beneficiaries. The former are the person or persons who take the trust principal remaining when the trust terminates. The instrument may authorize the trustee to pay out some or all of the principal to the latter, who are usually also income beneficiaries.

When the trust terminates, the underlying principal must be distributed in outright ownership. For example, in a tax-qualified marital trust, created for the benefit of a widow, the widow must receive all of the trust income at least annually, and may, but does not have to be, a discretionary principal invasion beneficiary. A marital trust usually terminates upon the death of the surviving spouse beneficiary—the widow, in our example—although a certain type of marital trust can continue in trust for secondary life beneficiaries, typically the settlor's children. The remainder of a marital trust usually passes outright to the creator's then surviving descendants. The assets of a tax-qualified marital trust are included in the taxable estate of the surviving spouse at her death, even though the trust property may not form a part of her distributable estate.

Per Stirpes and Per Capita

Almost all family trusts and wills distribute a trust's remainder to *issue per stirpes*, meaning "by the root." The term *issue* means all biological and adopted descendants. Per stirpes beneficiaries take the share that their deceased ancestor would have taken. *Issue per capita* means that all issue share equally regardless of their degree of consanguinity to the testator.

For instance, if a trust testator has two surviving children and two grandchildren born of a deceased child, with the trust remainder passing to the creator's issue per stirpes, the trust remainder would be divided into thirds, with one-third each going to the two living children and another third being shared equally (i.e., one-sixth each) by the two children of the deceased child.

If the disposition of the trust remainder were to the settlor's issue per capita, which today would be very unusual, the trust would be divided into four equal parts, and each of the two children and two grandchildren would receive an equal quarter interest.

Power to Invade Principal

A *principal invasion beneficiary*, who is usually also an income beneficiary, can be given portions of the trust principal, usually at the discretion of one or all of the trustees (or, in rare instances, a nontrustee "advisor") during the trust term. If a principal invasion beneficiary is also a trustee, the governing instrument, and sometimes state law, will often prohibit him from exercising the power to invade principal in his own favor.

Like the discretionary power to spray income, the power to invade principal may be without qualification or may be subject to some standard. An unqualified power might permit the trustee to give a beneficiary any part or all of the principal at any time, as he determines to be in the beneficiary's best interest, with or without consideration of the beneficiary's personal resources. This type of power is common; the only requirement is that the trustee not exercise it arbitrarily. The other choice is to permit the trustee to invade principal only in accordance with a specific, ascertainable standard spelled out in the instrument, such as the beneficiary's support and maintenance, medical and health needs, or education.

Trustees given discretionary powers to pay out trust income or principal must heed the standards spelled out in the trust instrument. Exercising this power usually means that one beneficiary, such as an income beneficiary receiving an invasion of principal, benefits, while another, typically the remainderman, loses. So trustees must comply fully with the income spray and principal invasion standards of such a trust. Failure to do so may constitute a breach of trust or a violation of the duty of impartiality.

Power of Appointment

A power of appointment permits its recipient, usually the income beneficiary, to designate who will receive the trust remainder, perhaps overriding those terms of the trust. There are two classes of powers of appointment: general, and special, or nongeneral. A general power gives the donee or holder of the power the right to give the trust property to anyone in the world, including his creditors, his estate, and his estate's creditors or even himself (such as through a power to withdraw). A general power of appointment is almost equivalent to full ownership of the property, and the Internal Revenue Service considers its holder as the owner for income and estate tax purposes. For trust law purposes, a general power of appointment is not title but only the power to designate the ultimate takers of the property, which is deemed to pass from the settlor or the testator and not the holder of the power, who is considered only a conduit.

A special power of appointment is limited in scope and may *not* be exercised in favor of the holder of the power, his creditors, his estate, or his estate's creditors, and it is *not* equivalent to ownership for tax or any other purpose. An example of language conferring a special power to convey the property would be "to such of my children and grandchildren as the donee of the power shall designate." The donee in this example would typically be the income beneficiary.

A power of appointment is exercisable by the holder of the power either during the term of the trust (a lifetime power), or upon the trust's termination (a testamentary power), or sometimes at both times. Usually the terms require the holder to make specific reference to the trust or will terms under which the power is granted, which avoids an unintentional exercise of the power or a question as to whether it was in fact exercised. If a donee of a power of appointment fails to exercise it in whole or part, the trust terms otherwise disposing of the principal will control.

A trustee must take note, before transferring the trust to the apparent remaindermen, that the holder of a power of appointment may have appointed the property elsewhere. Otherwise, he may be giving it to the wrong takers. It helps to use what is called a *refunding agreement* when distributing trust remainder property. Such agreements usually provide that the taker agrees to refund the property to the trustee if it is needed for expenses or claims against the trust that were unknown at termination. It can also be used to get the property back if it turns out that a holder of a power of appointment gave it to someone else.

Main Types of Trusts

As mentioned at the beginning of the chapter, trusts fall into two general classes: living and testamentary. Living trusts are created by an agreement between the settlor and a trustee. No court approval is necessary; the trustee derives his authority from the trust agreement and state law.

Testamentary

A testamentary trust is established by the testator's will, which takes effect only when probated (i.e., proved as authentic by a probate court).

Authority to approve the testator's choice of trustee lies with the probate court and is evidenced by a written permit or approval, usually called letters trusteeship.

By definition, any testamentary trust is irrevocable, because the settlor of the trust is no longer around to revoke it. However, because a trustee's discretionary powers to spray income or invade principal can affect the interests of the trust's income and remainder beneficiaries, he should exercise his discretionary power with the utmost caution, in conformity with his general duty to act impartially as among beneficiaries.

Living

Living or inter vivos trusts are either revocable or irrevocable. An irrevocable living trust is an unalterable transfer of an owner's property that creates immutable rights for those who are designated by the trust's governing instrument as income beneficiaries or remaindermen. Irrevocable trusts are used to make gifts of property when the donor chooses to benefit more than one donee, to divide interests in gifts, and to vary the times of enjoyment of the gift property rather than transfer present outright ownership.

A revocable living trust is used to manage the settlor's property during his life; it is not a gift. It usually continues after its creator's death, when it perforce becomes irrevocable, and to that extent substitutes for a will as to the property it holds. That property will not be part of the creator's probate estate, which is why revocable living trusts are often used to avoid probate, although *they do not avoid estate taxes*. Revocable trusts can also be used as a standby device to have a trustee available to handle the trust property if the settlor becomes incapacitated in the future. A common arrangement is for the settlor to act as sole trustee until death or incapacitation, when the successor trustee takes over. A person who creates a revocable trust and acts as trustee is still a fiduciary, and owes duties as a trustee to the future beneficiaries. A trust is a trust, and the settlor who is also a trustee of a revocable trust must never suppose that he is still an outright owner who can disregard the interests of the future beneficiaries.

Both irrevocable and revocable trusts are vehicles for the transmission of property from one generation to the next. The tax treatments of the two kinds of lifetime trusts are quite different. Our tax code treats a revocable trust as not involving a transfer of property, since the settlor retains all interest in it. Thus there is no gift tax when legal title to the property is transferred to the trust, and all income and capital gains are imputed to and taxed to the settlor.

An irrevocable trust involves a permanent transfer to the beneficiaries. So the settlor must pay gift tax on the transfer of property to the trust. Income paid out of the trust is taxed to the beneficiary who receives it. Income not paid out and accumulated by the trust, including realized capital gains, is taxed to the trust. In some irrevocable trusts, known as *grantor trusts*, income, including capital gains, is taxed to the settlor, usually by reason of certain powers reserved by the settlor over the trust.

A revocable trust is fully taxable upon the creator's death as part of the settlor's taxable estate because he still owned and controlled it when he died. An irrevocable trust is generally not included in the settlor's taxable estate, assuming he did not retain an interest in it, or a power to change its beneficial interests. Since the trust property was subject to gift tax when the irrevocable trust was created, no estate tax should be due when the settlor dies. If the trust is included in the settlor's taxable estate by reason, for example, of powers reserved by the settlor, the trustee may be responsible for paying the tax, depending on the tax apportionment clause in the settlor's will.

Specific Types of Irrevocable Trusts

Most trusts are irrevocable. They differ in their purposes and nomenclature but otherwise are similar. This section provides a brief synopsis of the more common types used in family planning, in addition to the revocable trusts we have just described.

Marital Deduction Trusts These trusts are for the benefit of a spouse and are designed to be exempt from the federal gift or estate tax by virtue of marital estate and gift tax deductions. Many states provide the same deductions. There is a special type of marital trust for spouses who are not U.S. citizens.

1. **"Qtips,"** or "qualified terminable interest property" marital deduction trusts. The spouse receives all the trust income for life, but the

trust designates who will receive property upon his or her death. These trusts are used by individuals who want to benefit a spouse but still control the disposition of the fund upon his or her death.

2. **General power of appointment trusts.** These are marital deduction trusts in which the surviving spouse beneficiary has the power over the disposition of the property upon his or her death, unlike a Qtip marital trust.

3. **Estate trusts.** These are rarely used marital deduction trusts which provide that when the spouse dies, the trust property will pass to his or her spouse's estate.

4. **Qdots.** These are federal marital deduction trusts for the benefit of spouses who are not U.S. citizens.

Credit Shelter Trusts These trusts (also called *bypass trusts*) are designed to take advantage of a U.S. taxpayer's unified credit allowed against U.S. gift or estate tax. Many states have similar credits. Typically, an individual creates a credit shelter trust for a spouse. By virtue of the unified credit, there is no gift or estate tax on the creation of the trust, which typically terminates on the death of the spouse, when the property passes to the children free of estate tax. Such a trust can be created during the settlor's lifetime, although it is more typically created by will.

Generation-Skipping Transfer Tax Trusts The generation-skipping transfer (GST) tax is a flat tax of 55 percent on any transfer to a grandchild or more remote descendant. Each U.S. taxpayer has a $1 million exemption from this tax. A GST exemption trust, often called a *dynasty trust,* takes advantage of this exemption by transferring up to that amount to a trust for grandchildren and more remote descendants. The trust property passes to future generations without transfer tax. The dynasty nomenclature derives from the custom of having GST exemption trusts last as long as state law permits before the property vests. In some states, this can be as long as ninety-five years.

Trusts for Minors These are living trusts established for minors, which qualify for the annual gift tax exclusion of $10,000 (or $20,000 if the other spouse consents). The trust can be made to last until the minor reaches age twenty-one (and even beyond if the child has the right to withdraw the trust principal).

Charitable Trusts
1. **Split interest trusts.** These are trusts in which both charitable and noncharitable beneficiaries have interests. There are two types:

    A. **Charitable remainder trusts.** Payments are made to an individual beneficiary or beneficiaries during the term of the trust. In an annuity trust, the payments are a fixed yearly sum. In a unitrust, the yearly payments are a fixed percentage of the fair market value of the trust fund, calculated annually. At the end of the term the trust principal passes to charity.

    B. **Charitable lead trusts.** Payments are made to charity during the term of the trust. Like the remainder trust, the lead trust can be an annuity trust or a unitrust. At the end of the term, the trust property passes to the remaindermen.

2. **Pure charitable trusts.** These trusts are solely for the benefit of charity, with no split interest for a noncharitable beneficiary.

Grantor Retained Annuity Trust In a grantor retained annuity trust (GRAT), the grantor (i.e., the settlor) retains the right to receive a fixed annuity payment for a fixed term of years. When the term ends, the trust property passes to other individuals, typically children.

Grantor Retained Unitrust A grantor retained unitrust (GRUT) is similar to a GRAT, except that the grantor retains the right to receive yearly payments of a fixed percentage of the trust assets during the trust term.

Irrevocable Life Insurance Trust Life insurance is generally subject to estate tax in the estate of the owner of the policy. However, life insurance can be purchased by or assigned to an irrevocable life insurance trust; this shelters the insurance proceeds from the estate tax that would occur if the owner of the policy died while owning it.

Pourover Trust A pourover trust is a revocable trust that is a receptacle for the transfer of probate property under a will. The trust may be unfunded;

it is then dormant until it receives the pourover property, or it can be funded for the benefit of the settlor during his life and receive a pourover from the will at his death.

Duties of a Trustee

Becoming a private trustee is a serious and burdensome undertaking, not merely a gesture of respect to a friend or loved one. One cannot hope to fulfill a trustee's duties without a solid grasp of both the governing general principles of trusts and the terms of the particular document.

A trustee's duties derive from the law and the terms of the trust. They take effect only when he accepts, either by signing a trust agreement or by accepting his designation by the probate court in a trust created by a will. Upon acceptance, a trustee assumes a duty to the beneficiaries to administer the trust in accordance with the rules of trusteeship, developed by state legislatures and courts over time. A violation of any of these rules constitutes a breach of trust, for which he can be personally liable.

The following summaries of trustee duties are extracted from the *Restatement of the Law Third, Trusts,* a compendium of trust law promulgated by the American Law Institute (hereinafter *Third Restatement*). They interact with each other and tie in with a trust's investment duties, which are discussed later. None stands in isolation.

Duty to Exercise Reasonable Care, Skill, and Caution

The trustee is under a duty to the beneficiary in administering the trust to exercise such care and skill as a man of ordinary prudence would exercise in dealing with his own property; and if a trustee has or procures his appointment as trustee by representing that he has greater skill than that of a man of ordinary prudence, he is under a duty to exercise such skill.

This rule makes a trustee liable for a loss that results from the failure to use the care and skill of a man of ordinary prudence, even though he might have acted in good faith and used all the care and skill of which he was capable. In other words, it is not enough to do the best you can; the test requires the care and skill that an ordinary prudent person would exercise. This is an *objective* standard. Its definition depends on a trust's particular circumstances.

The terms of a trust may relax or modify the duty of a trustee to exercise care and skill, although such modifications will be narrowly construed by the courts.

So what do "care, skill, and caution" mean? Generally, these elements can be defined as follows:

Care: A trustee's duty to inquire, examine, and investigate before taking action, being diligent and attentive to matters of the trust.

Skill: A trustee's duty either to have the necessary ability to handle the trust or to obtain it elsewhere.

Caution: A trustee's duty to preserve a trust's assets and to avoid speculation and recklessness.

The requirement of a trustee to act with care, skill, and caution is a standard of *conduct* rather than of outcome.

A trustee is under a duty to administer the trust solely in the interest of the beneficiaries. Loyalty is among the strictest of duties. It goes to the essence of the fiduciary relationship.

A trustee cannot profit in any way at the expense of the beneficiary without the beneficiary's consent, unless so authorized by the terms of the trust or by a proper court. This duty of loyalty is a prohibition against self-dealing by a trustee, even if acting in good faith, regardless of the fairness of the deal. The duty of loyalty requires avoidance of actual or potential conflicts of interests between a trustee and a beneficiary. For instance, a trustee may not buy trust property or sell his property to the trust; a trustee may not use trust property for his own benefit; a trustee may not disclose trust information that could harm a beneficiary to a third party.

Duty Not to Delegate

The trustee is under a duty to the beneficiary not to delegate to others the performance of acts which the trustee can reasonably be required to perform personally.

The traditional duty not to delegate has been the most controversial of all trustee rules, especially in the area of trust investments. It is based on the principle that a fiduciary's role is a personal one, and that personal duties should be performed by the fiduciary personally. It does admit certain limited exceptions. For example, it has been held proper for a trustee to delegate the performance of acts that he cannot reasonably be expected to perform personally, notably preparing tax returns, keeping trust accounts, collecting rents, or improving real property. In addition, delegating trust activities that by their very nature require professional skills or facilities that the trustee does not possess has been allowed.

Unfortunately, the traditional antidelegation rule fails to offer a clear-cut division between what is properly delegable and what is not. This stringent attitude has made trustees reluctant to stray far in delegating any duties, particularly investment duties, where the risk of loss is great.

Fortunately, after over 150 years of the "no delegation" rule, relief has arrived with the New Rule, which does permit delegation. This subject is so important that separate sections are devoted to it.

A note of caution: Authority to delegate under the New Rule is not automatic for all existing or future trusts, regardless of what the governing instrument may provide. The New Rule must first be adopted by the state in which the trust is established, or state law must at least authorize the delegation power. The authors expect all states to adopt the New Rule eventually. A mistake in this area can expose a trustee to serious liability.

Duty to Keep and Render Accounts

The trustee is under a duty to the beneficiary to keep and render clear accounts with respect to his administration.

The duty to keep and render accounts is intended to benefit not the trustee but the beneficiary. However, by fulfilling this duty a trustee can protect himself as well.

The trustee is to maintain a *book of accounts* that shows in detail the nature and amount of the trust property, *the income it produces,* and *all activity* relating to that property from the trust's inception to its termination. This is one of the most frequently neglected duties of individual trustees.

This duty also calls for the trustee to render accounts of the trust's activities to beneficiaries. Accountings by trustees are mostly a matter of state statutory rules, although some states allow the terms of the trust to dispense with accountings, or leave it to the trustees' discretion. Trustee accounts and court accountings are covered in a later chapter.

Duty to Take and Keep Control

The trustee is under a duty to the beneficiary to take reasonable steps to take and keep control of the trust property.

This duty does not mean that trustees must keep trust assets in their personal possession. Use of custodians and other agents is allowed, and will sometimes be the only prudent course.

Control, meaning exclusive control, is the key word. Unless the trust permits it, a beneficiary should not be allowed to hold trust property. As to securities, either the trustee must have them registered in his name or, if a bank or other custodian account is used, the trustee alone must have authority over the account. If the trustee receives or acquires an interest in property that cannot be physically held, he must personally hold the "indicia of ownership."

If possession is entrusted to a custodian or other agent, the trustee must act prudently in selecting him, arranging his duties and authority, and continuously monitoring his actions.

Duty to Preserve the Trust Property

The trustee is under a duty to the beneficiary to use reasonable care and skill to preserve the trust property.

As with the duty to manage investments prudently, preserving the trust property is a separate trustee duty. He must protect it from damage or loss of value, which may require insuring the property against fire, theft, and loss; safekeeping securities, particularly "bearer" securities; and keeping property, such as buildings, art, furniture, and the like, in good repair.

Some states have extended the duty to preserve trust property to include the duty to maintain purchasing power. The value of securities and other assets can be diminished by inflation. In the past, the Restatement did not require a trust to maintain the *real* or purchasing power value of property, as opposed to its *nominal* or stated value. *This policy has been changed by the New Rule.*

Duties to Enforce Claims and Defend Actions

The trustee is under a duty to the beneficiary to take reasonable steps to realize on claims that he holds in trust.

The trustee is under a duty to the beneficiary to defend actions that may result in a loss to the trust estate, unless under all the circumstances it is reasonable not to make such defense.

A trustee can easily overlook claims he may have as legal titleholder to the property. A successor trustee, for example, has a duty to obtain an account of his predecessor's activities, to ascertain whether any surcharge claims exist for possible past imprudent actions. A testamentary trustee appointed by will has a duty to obtain an account of the executor's actions, to ensure that the trust receives all the property it is entitled to, and to redress any breach of duty committed by the executor. A claim may exist regarding an investment, such as a bond default or a custodian's failure to collect and remit dividends.

The duty to enforce claims is tempered by allowing a trustee to determine their collectibility and to consider the expense of collecting as compared with the probability of recovery.

Similarly, if a trust is sued, a trustee has the duty to defend the suit and, if the trust loses, to appeal the decision, unless under the circumstances that course is unreasonable. A trustee can properly compromise or arbitrate a claim filed by or against a trust. However, he should not agree to arbitrate a claim if doing so would have the effect of waiving a trust's right to litigate. This issue can arise if an investment account agreement requires arbitration. Accepting such a waiver can be deemed a breach of trust if it deprives the trust of legal rights.

Duty to Keep Trust Property Separate

The trustee is under a duty to the beneficiary to keep the trust property separate from his individual property, and, so far as it is reasonable that he should do so, to keep it separate from property not subject to the trust, and to see that the property is designated as property of the trust.

This duty is especially important for investments. Commingling of a trustee's personal assets with the assets of a trust is improper. Also, where a trustee administers more than one trust, it is improper to mingle their property, despite convenience and economy.

All trust bank accounts, deeds to real estate, registered stock and bond certificates, and similar assets should ordinarily be identified as trust property, with the name of the trustee and the trust as the identifier, but not with the name of the trustee alone.

Of course, the paperless environment has altered the methods of securities transactions and registration, and given rise to special state legislation to permit current electronic book entry systems.

Duty to Make the Trust Property Productive

The trustee is under a duty to the beneficiary to use reasonable care and skill to make the trust property productive.

The trustee must manage the trust property so as to produce a reasonable income for the income beneficiary and to preserve the value of the corpus for the remainderman. Leaving large sums of cash uninvested is a violation of this duty. Similarly, unless the terms of a trust provide otherwise, a trustee who retains unimproved real estate without seeking ways to make it produce income may well be failing in his duty.

Summary

This catalog of trustee duties is not exhaustive and represents only those of special importance. Many trustees view their job as more modest than it really is.

Prudence in Perspective

The Meaning of Prudence

Prudence is a process, not a result. A trustee must act prudently in all he does for a trust and its beneficiaries.

Prudence is a flexible and unspecific standard of care, permitting wide discretion within general rules. It lacks the "safe harbor" features found in some other regulatory areas, such as federal securities and tax law, which tell you exactly what you should do.

Care, Skill, and Caution

The principle of prudence consists of the three elements, care, skill, and caution.

Administrative prudence means exercising care, skill, and caution in safekeeping trust assets, disposing of trust income and principal, maintaing trust records and keeping beneficiaries informed, and treating beneficiaries impartially.

There is also *investment prudence,* which means exercising care, skill, and caution when dealing with any aspect of a trust's investments. For instance, before investing any funds, a trustee should establish investment objectives that suit the purposes of the trust and needs of the beneficiaries; act diligently in selecting investments; determine the risk tolerance of a trust and choose only investments that suit that risk level; diversify the trust's holdings; focus on the portfolio's liquidity; determine whether to ask the advice of experts; and make certain that the investments themselves are advantageous to both the income and the remainder beneficiaries.

It helps greatly in understanding the new Prudent Investor Rule to see how it evolved from the old Prudent Man Rule, so we include a section to elucidate that background.

The Old Prudent Man Rule: *Harvard v. Amory*

The new Prudent Investor Rule, the subject of this book, derives from the old Prudent Man Rule. The Old Rule arose from a celebrated 1830 Massachusetts court decision, *Harvard College v. Amory.* Amory was a trustee of a $50,000 testamentary trust. The income went to the decedent's widow for life. At her death the remainder passed to Harvard and Massachusetts General Hospital in equal shares. The will gave Amory broad power to invest the trust fund, including in stocks according to "his best judgment and discretion." Amory invested the entire $50,000 fund in stocks that yielded 8 percent in dividends. Five years after the trust was established, the widow died. Amory filed his account with the court, showing a trust value of only $38,000. When he asked the court for his discharge, Harvard and Massachusetts General Hospital objected, demanding that he restore the $12,000 of lost capital. Judge Putnam, who heard the case, ruled in favor of Amory. The keystone of his decision was a phrase that has become graven in trust lore: "Do what you will, the capital is at hazard." He went on to pronounce a legal principle that became a universal standard for fiduciary conduct, known as the "Prudent Man Rule":

> All that can be required of a trustee to invest, is, that he shall conduct himself faithfully and exercise a sound discretion. He is to observe

how men of prudence, discretion, and intelligence manage their own affairs, not in regard to speculation, but in regard to the permanent disposition of their funds, considering the probable income, as well as the probable safety of the capital to be invested.

Over the next century the philosophies of state legislatures and courts changed from favoring flexibility in trust investing to a desire for more certainty and conservatism. In the first half of the twentieth century, most states enacted lists of specific types of investments that trustees were permitted to make, and courts established a series of subrules on what was prudent and what was not. Thus the flexibility and discretion of *Harvard v. Amory* rule gave way to rules and restrictions.

The following are some examples of restrictions tacked on to the Old Rule by state courts and legislatures:

- Certain types of investments were imprudent per se and thus not allowed for trusts.

- Each investment in a trust portfolio, rather than the portfolio as a whole, had to satisfy the tests of prudence.

- A trustee was required to perform duties personally, not delegate them to others.

- Investment in mutual funds or index funds was an improper delegation of duty by the trustee.

The various restrictions grafted onto *Harvard v. Amory* by state legislatures and courts ultimately impaired its value by reducing its flexibility. They tended to backtrack toward earlier conservative and protective theories of trust investing, although not without struggles. Some institutions attempted to buck the restrictive trend by adopting model language echoing Judge Putnam's opinion.

In 1942 the American Bankers Association promulgated its Model Prudent Man Investment Statute, which both parroted and slightly modified Judge Putnam's words:

In acquiring, investing, reinvesting, exchanging, retaining, selling, and managing property for the benefit of another, a fiduciary shall exercise the judgment and care under the circumstances then prevailing, which men of prudence, discretion, and intelligence exercise in the management of their own affairs, not in regard to speculation but in regard to the permanent disposition of their funds, considering the probable income as well as probable safety of their capital.

In 1959 the *Restatement of the Law, Trusts* (Second)—the Bible of American trust law principles—used different language with the same impact:

In making investments of trust funds the trustee is under a duty to the beneficiary in the absence of provisions in the terms of the trust or of a statute otherwise providing, to make such investments and only such investments as a prudent man would make of his own property having in view the preservation of the estate and the amount and regularity of the income to be derived.

In 1972 the National Conference of Commissioners on Uniform State Laws issued a model Uniform Management of Institutional Funds (*not* private trusts) Act, which at this writing has been adopted by many states. This model legislation imposed a variation of the Prudent Man Rule on trustees and directors of not-for-profit institutions such as universities, hospitals, museums, and charitable foundations.

As recently as 1974, the National Conference of Commissioners on Uniform State Laws adopted the following wording for its Uniform Probate Code Prudent Man Rule:

Except as otherwise provided by the terms of the trust, the trustee shall observe the standards in dealing with the trust assets that would be observed by a prudent man dealing with the property of another, and if the trustee has special skills or expertise, he is under duty to use those skills.

Also in 1974, Congress rejected many of these restrictive subrules when it enacted the Employee Retirement Income Security Act (ERISA), governing employee benefit trusts. ERISA incorporated its own prudent man rule, adopting many recommendations of the legal and investment communities. In its formulation, Congress sought to "avoid repeating the mistake of freezing its rules against future learning and developments." Its prudent man section states:

> The fiduciary shall discharge his duties with the care, skill, prudence, and diligence under the circumstances then prevailing that a prudent man acting in a like capacity and familiar with such matters would use in the conduct of an enterprise of a like character and with like aims; and by diversifying the investments of the plans so as to minimize the risk of large losses, unless under the circumstances it is clearly prudent not to do so.

Over time the states' additions and restrictions had resulted in so many prohibitions that trust investing departed from how the real-life prudent man was handling his own investments—the heart of the Old Rule! By the late 1950s, the *accretions* to the Rule *became* the Rule. In reaction to the restrictive court rulings and legislation, a counterreformation arose. The trust industry and the legal profession disagreed with the ultraconservatism of the modified Rule. Feminism influenced a name change to the "Prudent Person Rule." Lawyers countered its strictures by writing investment powers into wills and trust agreements that authorized the trustee to invest in his sole discretion, without regard to state law restrictions, even if the securities were non-income-producing, unseasoned, or speculative, essentially drafting out the constricting parts of a state's Prudent Man Rule. Some banks included in their specimen clauses for wills and trusts a provision that the trustee could invest in any securities that were eligible for the bank's own investment management accounts. Some drafters of wills and trusts allowed the trustee to invest in "alternative investments, such as venture capital, covered options, precious metals and natural resources."

Eventually, the entire trust community accepted the view that the old Prudent Man Rule placed trusts at a disadvantage by depriving them of newer investment variations. State legislatures began to join the movement, eliminating the legal lists that dictated what trusts could invest in, and replacing them with Prudent Man standards similar to *Harvard v. Amory*. In 1970 New York State adopted the following Prudent Man Rule:

> A fiduciary holding funds for investment may invest the same in such securities as would be acquired by prudent men of discretion and intelligence in such matters who are seeking a reasonable income and preservation of their capital, provided, however, that nothing in

this subparagraph shall limit the effect of any will, agreement court order or other instrument creating or defining the investment powers of a fiduciary, or shall restrict the authority of a court of proper jurisdiction to instruct the fiduciary in the interpretation or administration of the express terms of any will, agreement or other instrument or in the administration of the property under the fiduciary's care.

Finally, in 1994 the National Conference of Commissioners of Uniform State Laws published its Uniform Prudent Investor Act, with the stated purpose of updating private trust investment law "in recognition of the alterations that have occurred in investment practice. . ." This Act draws upon the revised standards for prudent trust investment promulgated by the American Law Institute in its Third Restatement (1992), Section 227. It reads as follows:

The trustee is under a duty to the beneficiaries to invest and manage the funds of the trust as a prudent investor would, in light of the purposes, terms, distribution requirements, and other circumstances of the trust.

a. This standard requires the exercise of reasonable care, skill, and caution, and is to be applied to investments not in isolation but in the context of the trust portfolio and as a part of an overall investment strategy, which should incorporate risk and return objectives reasonably suitable to the trust.

b. In making and implementing investment decisions, the trustee has a duty to diversify the investments of the trust unless, under the circumstances, it is prudent not to do so.

c. In addition, the trustee must:

1. conform to fundamental fiduciary duties of loyalty and impartiality;

2. act with prudence in deciding whether and how to delegate authority and in the selection and supervision of agents; and

3. incur only costs that are reasonable in amount and appropriate to the investment responsibilities of the trusteeship.

d. The trustee's duties under this Section are subject to the rule of § 228, dealing primarily with contrary investment provisions of a trust or statute.

The Old Rule, lumbered with so many restrictions over the years, was thus finally freed up.

The New Prudent Investor Rule

The American Law Institute's 1992 *Restatement of the Law Third, Trusts* is not itself the law, but it is the definitive commentary on the law. Lawyers, professional trustees, and the courts often turn to it for guidance. It has greatly influenced the development of American trust law.

The sponsors of the Third Restatement concluded that the inflexibility imposed by the courts had placed unjustified liability upon trustees and inhibited the exercise of investment judgment. The American Law Institute's reporter says that the New Rule liberates expert trustees "to pursue challenging, rewarding, nontraditional strategies" and provides unsophisticated trustees with reasonably clear guidance to practical courses of investment.

So the essence of the New Rule is that no investments or techniques are imprudent per se—a radical departure, considering that the Old Rule held that investments that were speculative or non-income-producing were intrinsically imprudent.

The New Rule contains five basic principles:

1. Diversification is fundamental to risk minimization and is therefore ordinarily required of trustees.

2. Risk and return are so directly related that trustees have a duty to analyze and make conscious decisions concerning the levels of risk appropriate to the purposes of the trust.

3. Trustees have a duty to avoid fees, transaction costs, and other expenses that are not justified by the objectives of the investment program.

4. The fiduciary's duty of impartiality requires a conscious balancing of current income and growth.

5. Trustees may have a duty, as well as the authority, to delegate as prudent investors would.

The Third Restatement's new Prudent Investor Rule is intended for a trust only if it is consistent with the terms of a trust and with state law. Generally, the terms of the trust will control. Assuming that a state has adopted the New Rule, or permits a trust to adopt it, then the terms of the trust will dictate whether the New Rule applies to its investment activity.

The terms of a trust may expand or limit the provisions of the Third Restatement's New Rule. In general, a trustee can properly make investments as expressly or implicitly authorized by the terms of the trust. Thus a trust's terms will control a trustee's investment duties and authorities, even if different from the Rule, so long as they do not conflict with the law. But absent contrary provisions (or silence) in the terms of the trust, the Restatement's New Rule will govern, if a state has adopted it.

While the Restatement mainly addresses the administration of private trusts, it is also generally appropriate to charitable or public funds. The New Rule is also intended to guide executors and administrators of estates, guardians, conservators, and the like.

Even though the Restatement's New Rule does not directly apply to nonprivate trustees, it is the safest route for them to follow, since courts and regulators who supervise these other fiduciaries will probably turn to the Restatement for guidance, just as they looked to the previous Restatement in the days of the Old Rule.

Duty to Conform to General Fiduciary Standards

Of the standards to which a trustee must adhere, the most important are that he must exercise care, skill, and caution, and must manifest loyalty and impartiality. His compliance with these duties is judged as of the time an investment decision is made, and *not* with the benefit of hindsight or subsequent developments, nor on the outcome of his investment decisions. This is just as it was under Judge Putnam's rule.

Loyalty means that a trustee must be free of conflicts of interest in managing a trust's investments, and must act solely in the interests of the beneficiaries. Impartiality means that a trustee must recognize the divergent interests of different beneficiaries. He must resolve these differences "in a fair and reasonable manner," whatever that may mean.

Care includes obtaining relevant information on the circumstances and requirements of the trust and its beneficiaries, on the contents and resources of the trust estate, and about the available investment choices. The duty of care may also require a trustee to seek the advice of others.

Skill means that although a person of ordinary intelligence, without financial experience, may serve as a trustee, he should obtain the guidance of specialists in order to meet the skill criterion. Furthermore, unlike the Old Rule, which in general forbade investment delegation, the Restatement holds that a trustee may in some instances have a duty to delegate investment authority to others. In so delegating, "the trustee must exercise appropriate care and skill in selecting and supervising agents and in determining the degree and terms of the delegation." If, on the other hand, a trustee possesses more than ordinary skill, he must use it.

The New Rule requires caution when investing trust funds, with a view to both safety of capital and securing a reasonable return. Safety of capital includes preserving its real, as against nominal, value; that is, seeking to limit the erosion of the trust's purchasing power due to inflation.

In a major departure from the Old Rule, the New Rule defines reasonable return as *total return*: capital growth as well as income. Furthermore, under the New Rule, capital growth does not necessarily mean only preservation of the trust's purchasing power but may extend to growth in the real value of principal in appropriate cases.[1] The Restatement continues:

> In balancing the return objectives between flow of income and growth of principal, emphasis depends not only on the purposes and distribution requirements of the trust, but also on its other circumstances and specific terms, such as the beneficiaries' tax positions and whether the trustee has power to invade principal.

---

[1] We note that this is a remarkable line of reasoning. It is in reality quite enough to preserve buying power in real terms while providing a reasonable income that rises to offset inflation. Seeking much more than this—swinging for the fences—may achieve much less. Nevertheless, says the New Rule, it is permissible to try, if this endeavor is consistent with the situation of the trust. And these days many of the finest growth companies pay very low dividends, while rewarding their shareholders by reducing the number of shares outstanding through open-market purchases.

Caution and Risk Management

The Old Rule requires caution in making investments. This has been interpreted as a duty to avoid speculation and undue risk and follows from the "risk-averse" duty of caution.

That duty survives under the New Rule, but it is altered. After declaring that all investments, even U.S. Treasury obligations, and all investment strategies involve some risk, the Restatement asserts that the duty of caution does not call for the total avoidance of risk by trustees but rather for its "prudent management," taking account of inflation, volatility, illiquidity, and the like, in addition to potential loss.

This emphasis on active risk management in trusts is new. Its importance is shown by its specific inclusion in the Restatement's phrase "an overall investment strategy, which should incorporate risk and return objectives reasonably suitable to the trust." Risk management by a trustee is viewed by the Restatement as requiring that careful attention be given to each trust's particular "risk tolerance," defined as its tolerance for volatility, given the needs of the beneficiaries. Under the New Rule, the trustee has an affirmative duty to assess its risk tolerance and actively manage the risk element of its investments.

Diversification

The Restatement declares:

> In making and implementing investment decisions, the trustee has a duty to diversify the investments of the trust unless, under the circumstances, it is prudent not to do so.

This duty was included as a separate one in the preceding Second Restatement, but not as part of that edition's prudent investment standard. In the Third Restatement, the duty is elevated to the standard itself, to show "its centrality in fiduciary investing," and perhaps to encourage the states to adopt diversification as a requirement in their Prudent Investor statutes. Strange as it seems, trust portfolio diversification has not always been mandated by state law, even though it has for many years been almost universally followed in trust portfolios.

The Third Restatement also declares that "no objective, general legal standard can be set for a degree of risk that is or is not prudent," and it acknowledges that "the degree of risk permitted for a particular trust is ultimately a matter for interpretation and judgment. This requires that a trustee make reasonable efforts to ascertain the purposes of the trust and to understand the types of investments suitable to those purposes in light of all the relevant circumstances."

The Uniform Prudent Investor Act

The Third Restatement is dedicated exclusively to the *investment* and related duties of trustees. Based on its new Prudent Investor Rule, another institution, the National Conference of Commissioners on Uniform State Laws, whose charter is to promote uniformity among the fifty states in certain areas of the law, in 1994 promulgated the Uniform Prudent Investor Act, which we will call the Model Act.

Many states responded to the Model Act by revising their Prudent Man statutes to conform to the Act. Others adopted the entire Model Act with only slight modifications (see Appendix 6).

The Model Act is the wave of the future. All trustees of private trusts must understand its provisions, even trustees in states that have not yet adopted it. To that end we will describe its more important sections.

Like the Third Restatement from which it flows, the Model Act makes five fundamental changes in the old rules governing private trust investing:

1. The standard of prudence applies to the trust portfolio as a whole, rather than to each individual investment on its own.

2. The trade-off between investment risk and return is the fiduciary's central consideration.

3. All specific restrictions on the types of investments that a trustee may use are abrogated; a trustee may invest in anything that plays an appropriate role in achieving the risk/return objectives of the trust and that meets the requirements of prudent investing.

4. The traditional duty to diversify investments is integrated into the Prudent Investment Standard.

5. Delegation by a trustee is permissible, subject to certain safeguards.

For the text of the Model Act, see Appendix 4.

Summary of the Model Act

The heart of the Model Act is its Section 2, setting forth a new standard of prudence to which the trustees it governs must adhere, unless the trust instrument provides otherwise. The Act's prudence standard provides that

a. A trustee shall invest and manage trust assets as a prudent investor would, by considering the purpose, terms, distribution requirements, and other circumstances of the trust. In satisfying this standard, the trustee shall exercise reasonable care, skill, and caution.

b. A trustee's investment and management decisions respecting individual assets must be evaluated not in isolation but in the context of the trust portfolio as a whole and as a part of an overall investment strategy having risk and return objectives reasonably suited to the trust.

Risk/Reward

The Act incorporates a risk-reward ratio concept into the Model Act's new Prudence Standard. A Comment invokes "the main theme of modern investment practice, sensitivity to the risk/return curve." The Comment explains that risk varies with financial and other circumstances, and thus with a trust's purpose and the circumstances of the beneficiaries.

Strategy

A trustee must (1) develop an overall portfolio strategy designed to achieve expected present and future distributions to its beneficiaries and (2) do so with proper regard for risk and return. Unlike the Old Rule's focus on the prudence of individual investment holdings and avoiding risk, the new standard recognizes the relationship of the potential for reward to a trust from accepting risk and focuses on the trustee's duty to manage that risk over the portfolio as a whole, not taking each holding in isolation. This departure is a most noteworthy feature of the Model Act and New Rule.

The Act identifies *key factors* that a trustee should consider when investing and managing trust assets, notably:

- General economic conditions

- The possible effect of inflation or deflation

- The expected tax consequences for the beneficiaries of investment decisions or strategies

- The role that each investment or course of action plays within the overall trust portfolio

- The expected total return from income and capital appreciation

- The beneficiaries' other resources

- Needs for liquidity, regularity of income, and preservation or appreciation of capital

- An asset's special relationship or special value, if any, to the purposes of the trust or to the beneficiaries

The Model Act further states a trustee need not satisfy all of these factors for each investment but only those "as are relevant to the trust or its beneficiaries."

The Model Act also includes three *investment policy* provisions:

1. A trustee shall make a reasonable effort to verify the facts relevant to the investment and management of trust assets.

2. A trustee may invest in any kind of property or type of investment consistent with the standards of the Act.

3. A trustee possessing special skills or expertise, or who is selected as trustee based upon the representation of having such skills, has a duty to use those special skills or expertise.

The first provision invokes a trustee's traditional duty to investigate before investing; that is, to analyze information likely to bear on an investment's value or safety. Examples offered are financial reports, auditor's reports, records of title, and the like—routine steps taken by investment analysts.

The second, in a major change for trustees of private trusts, declares the policy that no kind of property or investment is inherently imprudent. Under the Old Rule a variety of investments had been categorized by the courts as imprudent, such as venture capital, futures, options, lower-rated bonds, and stocks of new and untried enterprises. Conversely, the Model Act's Commentary also points out that long-term bonds, which were historically considered ideal for trusts, are now thought to incur a level of risk and volatility perhaps inappropriate for some trusts.

In underscoring its belief that no specific investments or techniques should be deemed imprudent per se, the Model Act's Commentary opines that trust beneficiaries are better protected by the Act's emphasis on close attention to risk/return objectives than by an attempt to predict categories of investment that are intrinsically imprudent. The Act espouses the view that the trustee's task is to invest at a risk level suitable to the purposes of the trust, whether that level is speculative or conservative.

The third provision reaffirms a policy of the old Prudent Man Rule. That policy distinguished between amateur and professional trustees, holding that the standard of prudence is "relational," meaning that the standard for professional trustees is higher than that for laymen.

Diversification

The Model Act and the Third Restatement both emphasize the importance of diversification to reduce risk in a trust portfolio. A trustee should diversify a trust's investments unless, owing to special circumstances, he reasonably determines that the purposes of the trust are better served by putting most of his eggs in a single basket. They even acknowledge that there is no automatic rule or method for identifying how much diversification is enough.

The duty to diversify might not apply if a trust held a block of low-basis stock, where the capital gains tax cost of selling it would outweigh the benefit of diversifying, or if by selling a stock the trust would lose control of a business.

Initial Review

The Act provides that the trustee of a new trust, or of an old trust to which new assets are being added, or a successor trustee, should conduct a review immediately and decide whether to retain or dispose of those assets. This provision applies to investments that were suitable when acquired but subsequently became unsuitable. The provision derives from the Restatement's admonition that a trustee must constantly monitor a trust's investments.

Loyalty

The Model Act includes a separate section on the duty of loyalty, which it calls "the most characteristic rule of trust law," namely to "invest and manage the trust assets solely in the interest of the beneficiaries."

Impartiality

Another traditional duty, also subject to a separate section in the Model Act, is the duty of a trustee to act impartially, taking into account any differing interests of the beneficiaries, whether successive, such as income beneficiaries and remaindermen, or simultaneous, as within a class of income beneficiaries.

This duty is the hardest for a trustee to fulfill to all the beneficiaries' satisfaction. It often forces him to adopt compromise investment strategies: to play it safe as between an income beneficiary wanting high income and prospective remaindermen wanting high growth. The supposed failure to meet this duty of impartiality often gives rise to remaindermens' claims when the trust terminates that the trustee violated the impartiality duty by giving the income beneficiaries too much income.

Some trusts avoid the problem by eliminating the duty of impartiality. For example, if the settlor's widow is the income beneficiary, and clearly the preferred beneficiary, and if the testator wants the trustee to pursue a high-income investment strategy, he can simply relieve the trustee of the duty to be impartial vis-à-vis the remaindermen. A fine solution is to distribute 4 percent a year, say, of the running three-year average total capital.

Costs

The Act provides that a trustee may only incur costs that are appropriate and reasonable. Trustees are thus obliged to make comparisons on transaction and agent costs such as brokerage commissions, and to calculate the cost-benefit ratio, considering the trust's size and ability to bear such costs. These costs include the trustee's own compensation. Although he has a duty to *control* costs, a trustee is not obliged to pay only the *lowest* costs.

The Model Act preserves the time-honored principle that compliance with the Prudent Investor Rule is to be determined in light of the circumstances at the time of the trustee's action, not by hindsight. A trustee is not an insurer or guarantor.

Delegation

A key feature of the Model Act breaks with the past and permits a trustee to delegate investment and management functions that he previously had to perform personally if a prudent investor with similar skills would reasonably delegate them under the circumstances. Still, a trustee must act prudently in the following:

- Selecting the agent

- Establishing the scope and terms of the delegation

- Periodically reviewing the agent's actions

An agent who accepts delegation by a trustee is subject to the jurisdiction of the courts of the state in which the trust is resident.

The Model Act provides that a trustee who complies with its requirements for delegating investment and management functions to an agent will *not* be liable to the beneficiaries or to the trust for the agent's decisions or actions. Not every state is likely to accept this provision. New York's version of the Model Act, for instance, omits it.

The Model Act provides that it shall apply to trusts in existence upon, and created after, the date it is enacted by an adopting state. As to existing trusts, it applies only to investment decisions and actions made after its effective date.

Managing a Trust Under the New Rule

Procedures

Prudence Is Conduct

The most positive features of the New Rule are its flexibility and lack of specific prohibitions. Prudence is a process. But what about a trustee who wants to know if the investment or course of action he contemplates will be deemed prudent when a judge studies it years later? The Third Restatement, the source of the Rule, speaks thus:

> There are no universally accepted and enduring theories of financial markets or prescriptions for investment that can provide clear and specific guidance to trustees and courts. Varied approaches to the prudent investment of trust funds are therefore permitted by the law.

Given this flexibility, trustees who want to protect themselves must be able to *show that they acted prudently*. Yet the increase in authority conveyed by the New Rule carries increased responsibility. This chapter offers a framework for a trust management system that trustees can adopt to help show they discharged their investment responsibilities prudently.

Understand the Purposes and Terms

First, understand and clearly state the trust's objectives. Never assume that the objectives are what you think they should be. Analyze the trust document and pay close attention to its particular objectives. If necessary, seek legal advice to interpret the settlor's intent. In some cases—and they are mercifully rare—that intent may be so ambiguous as to require a court to construe its terms.

Understand and clearly state the needs of the beneficiaries. For many reasons, a trustee is well advised to interview each beneficiary in turn, if possible with their advisors present, and to make note of such crucial facts as tax brackets, outside resources, and special financial needs. He should remind the beneficiaries to notify him in writing when their situations change. One should not manage a trust in a vacuum, even if the trust's investments are performing well.

Understand and clearly state the trustee's powers, the terms of the trust, and the local governing law. The trustee may well want to consult the lawyer who drafted the trust. The best time to do this is at the inception of his trusteeship. Ask the attorney to prepare a digest of the trust, which you can use as a ready reference. (Appendix 2 offers a sample digest.) Find out if the New Rule applies in your state. If not, you may not be able to delegate full discretionary investment authority to an investment advisor and will instead have to direct each transaction personally. Remember, an otherwise proper transaction or strategy cannot be executed if the trustee does not have the authority to use it because of restrictions under the trust instrument or state law. If, however, state law has embraced the New Rule, and the terms of a trust do not cut down its scope, the trustee need not be concerned about limitations on his investment powers. The focus, then, will be almost exclusively on meeting the trust's particular requirements.

Establish a Strategy and a System

Develop and clearly state an *overall plan* for managing the trust, and then stick to it. A "trust plan" should be developed in conjunction with the income beneficiary, the investment manager, and the trust's attorney. It should be reviewed regularly to determine any changes in the needs or other circumstances of the income beneficiary, the remaindermen, and investment developments. Trust management should be an active and dynamic process, not a passive and static one.

Execute all decisions in accord with a trustee's fundamental duties and the peculiar needs of the trust. Necessary skill must be applied or acquired and a risk-return analysis done *before* investment actions are taken. A trustee's records must demonstrate that care, skill, and caution were exercised at all times. An organized and disciplined approach lends the appearance and, one hopes, the substance of prudence. A seat-of-the-pants approach smacks of imprudence. The emphasis should be on demonstrating that one has adopted a clear, recognizable framework for managing the trust.

Document the trustee's decision-making process, whether or not the investment duty is being delegated. A paper trail, showing a full trust management system, is a lifesaver if a trustee is called upon to defend an investment loss. He must be able to show the following:

- The *rationale* for an investment transaction or strategy

- The *steps* taken in arriving at the decision, notably due diligence and responsiveness to trust objectives

- The *factors* he considered in developing a strategy and making a specific investment

The best way to accomplish this is to write memoranda to the trust's files, setting forth a summary of these three elements. Periodically, a trustee should make a record of his review of the investment strategy and the specific investments. If no changes are made, the record should indicate a conscious decision to maintain the status quo. If there are substantial changes, the trustee should make a written record of the reasons. This record should include reference to the trust's stated investment objectives, the method used to determine them, and the strategy adopted to achieve them.

Develop an orderly procedure for delegating duties to outside agents. Under the New Rule, a trustee can delegate to an investment manager, assuming state law and the trust instrument allow it, if the trustee does the following:

- Acts prudently in selecting the agent

- Carefully sets down the scope and terms of the delegation

- Monitors the agent's performance

Accordingly, a trust management system that includes delegation to outside agents should include these three requirements. When selecting an investment manager, the trustee will want to use screening processes similar to those employed by institutional investors. Appendix 9 offers a form that can be adapted for a private trust. The advisor's ADV Form must also be studied. An advisor should not be selected on the basis of investment performance alone. Trustees must also make certain that their agents are familiar with the New Rule.

The investment agent's standard form of agreement should embody the New Rule's standards of care, rather than the lower standard usually found in investment agreements. For example, the trustee should not agree to be bound by arbitration for the settlement of disputes with the agent.

Also, standard periodic investment reports from the manager may satisfy the typical discretionary account for an individual, but they are not enough for a trust. A trustee should meet with the investment advisor at least once a year, and preferably more frequently. At the beginning of an account relationship, particularly if it is to give full discretion to the advisor, a trustee should meet several times to ensure that the scope and terms of the delegation are clearly understood. Both initial and ongoing meetings are necessary to assure the trustee that the investment manager grasps the special requirements of a fiduciary relationship, and the trust standard to which *both the trustee and the investment manager* are held.

Finally, a trustee who delegates the investment function will want to maintain careful records of his monitoring activities, complete enough to show he exercised prudence at all times.

A formal filing system helps demonstrate prudence, and of course a good filing system will facilitate administration of the trust. The foregoing steps can be separate sections of a trustee's filing system. He can add folders for correspondence, original trust and court documents, tax returns, accountings, inventories of trust assets, and receipts and releases for property distributions. Then he will have the makings of a professional trustee records mechanism.

A trustee must also demonstrate prudence by establishing and using a rational system that shows he conducted an analysis of the settlor's intent, the beneficiaries' needs, the purposes of the trust, and the investment objectives designed to achieve these concerns, including the risk-return aspects of an overall investment strategy. If called upon to determine whether the trustee acted prudently, a court will probably review this system.

Coping with Trustee Liability

A trustee is not a guarantor of his investment actions. An exception is when he makes an unauthorized investment, but this situation would be uncommon today because trustees are usually granted very broad powers of investment by modern trust documents.

However, by imposing a very high standard of care the New Rule may make it easier to establish trustee liability. If a breach of that standard—imprudence—causes a loss, the trustee can be held liable for the loss to the trust and to the beneficiaries. If there are multiple trustees, they are jointly and severally liable for an imprudent act of any one of the them. If the terms of the trust or state law permit more than two cotrustees to act by majority, the minority trustees are still exposed to loss, unless immunized by the terms of the trust or state law. If there are only two trustees, they must act unanimously, unless the trust provides otherwise. Only ministerial—nonjudgmental—tasks may be apportioned by cotrustees among themselves. Nevertheless, the trust terms can provide for specific allocation of duties among cotrustees, and a trustee may thus be absolved of a duty by the trust instrument. However, if a cotrustee is assigned a specific duty by a trust and is not performing that duty or is acting imprudently, the absolved trustee may have a duty to take corrective action.

A trust instrument may grant fiduciary powers to a trustee in excess of the powers authorized to trustees under state law. Courts have generally viewed exculpatory clauses in trust instruments unfavorably, but such clauses are generally enforced and are commonly used in living trust agreements; less so in testamentary trusts. State law may even prohibit them in wills as a matter of public policy. Such clauses generally operate to excuse a trustee from liability, except for willful misconduct or fraud. They can relieve a trustee of liability for negligence or failure to exercise sound judgment that would otherwise amount to imprudence or a breach of trust.

Public policy places limitations on such exoneration provisions. Generally a trustee may not be excused from liability for willful and deliberate violations of fiduciary obligations, including the duty to act with care, skill, and caution, nor for gross negligence, bad faith, or dishonesty, nor for acts of self-dealing except those specifically authorized by the trust or the beneficiaries. In other words, public policy sets a limit on actions or omissions beyond which a settlor may not relieve a trustee from liability for breach of fiduciary duty to a trust.

In addition, although many trusts grant the trustee the power to act with "absolute discretion," public policy limits that authority. A trustee may not exercise discretionary powers or authority dishonestly or in bad faith, regardless of contrary provisions in a trust document.

Finally, a trust instrument may not excuse a trustee from liability for failure to account in a court for his administration, nor may a trust defeat the right of a court to remove an unfit or incapacitated trustee, even if the settlor was aware of the trustee's condition when the trustee designation was made.

Trustees are obliged to prepare a formal accounting of their trusteeships. Accountings are either intermediate, meaning before a trust terminates, or final, at the trust's termination. When to account and be discharged—relieved of the duties and obligations of trusteeship—is generally left up to the trustee, unless state law permits a beneficiary to demand an accounting.

A trustee has the right to render an account of his or her trustee stewardship and to be discharged from any liability or responsibility for all actions fairly and fully disclosed in the accounting. In certain circumstances, beneficiaries also have the right to force a trustee to account for his actions as a trustee, even if the trust instrument dispenses with that duty.

Accountings are intended to inform beneficiaries, to provide a method for resolving questions about a trustee's activities, and to obtain his discharge, or his possible surcharge liability for losses sustained by the trust during the accounting period.

Trustee accountings are conclusive as to the actions of the trustee, assuming proper notice to beneficiaries and adequate disclosure. They may be reopened only by necessary parties who are not notified, if there was fraud or misrepresentation by the trustee. There is no statute of limitations for review of a trustee's fiduciary activities. The only way to close out his liability is through intermediate and final accountings and discharge of the trustee, or similar procedures authorized by state law.

When a trustee assumes his office as a successor rather than an original trustee, it becomes extremely important to have an accounting by his predecessor. Otherwise, depending on state law, the successor trustee could be held responsible for the acts of a predecessor who had not filed an accounting or been discharged.

A trustee is well advised to submit an accounting every ten years, and at least every twenty years. Also, an accounting is often appropriate when a major and special asset of the trust is sold, such as a family's closely held business.

An accounting trustee is generally exposed for realized, but not for unrealized, losses caused by his imprudent actions during the accounting period. Still, a beneficiary may question the retention of holdings with significant unrealized losses, and a trustee could be held liable if the court finds that the retention has been imprudent.

Each time a trustee accounts and proper disclosure and notice are given, the slate is wiped clean. The trustee's future responsibility for the trust assets is reset to their market value on the date of the accounting.

Specific Measures

What steps can one take, as a trustee, to avoid incurring personal liability for investment losses in the trust? Besides requesting exoneration in the trust document and having the settlor state clearly his priorities between the income beneficiaries and the remaindermen, the answer is to do things right.

• Master the fundamental duties of a trustee.

• Avoid even the semblance of self-dealing.

- Develop financial and tax profiles for each beneficiary.

- Record analyses of distribution liquidity needs.

- Take out fiduciary malpractice insurance.

- Develop *written* investment objectives.

- Engage any outside professionals under a systematic and detailed screening process, and monitor them carefully.

- *Record* risk-return analyses.

- *Record* your study of the impact of inflation or deflation.

- *Record* considerations of portfolio diversification to reduce the risk of large losses.

- Negotiate all costs at least down to standard levels.

- Avoid a pattern of considerable periods of inactivity.

- Minimize taxes.

- Avoid too many investment transactions.

- Be scrupulously fair as between income beneficiaries and remaindermen, and *record* your reasoning.

- Stay in touch with the beneficiaries, and have them ratify your actions in writing from time to time.

- Obtain cotrustee approvals.

- *Record* key actions and their rationale.

- In extreme cases, ask the advice and direction of a court.

- Account periodically to receive a discharge.

Trustee Compensation

A trustee may act with or without compensation, but the absence of compensation does not relieve him of his duties. Compensation of private trustees covers a range from zero (usual for family trustees) to state statutory rules for individual trustees. Bank trust departments generally publish fee schedules. Statutory rates of individual trustee compensation generally follow a graduated scale, cover a calendar year, and are based on the market value of the principal. Usually the fee is charged partly to the income account and partly to the trust principal so that the cost is borne by both income and remainder beneficiaries. The New York rule, for instance, allots one-third to income and two-thirds to principal, unless the trust provides otherwise.

An example of a state statutory fee schedule is New York's, which is as follows:

- On the first $400,000 of principal assets held in the trust, each trustee is entitled annually to $10.50 per $1,000, or 1.5 percent.

- On the next $600,000 of principal, $4.50 per $1,000, or 0.45 percent.

- On all amounts of principal in excess of $1,000,000, $3.00 per $1,000, or 0.3 percent.

Although New York has no maximum or minimum fee, there is a limit on the number of full statutory fees that can be paid by a trust with multiple trustees. In those cases the maximum fee can be shared equally or in proportion to the work performed by each trustee. A trust instrument can provide its own compensation schedule.

Other states simply provide that a trustee is to receive "reasonable compensation." The levels are developed by the local courts and become a community standard.

Banks and trust companies generally publish minimum annual fees and extraordinary fees for special services, such as supervising a closely held business, managing real estate, tax services, and the like.

In the absence of a state statutory fee scheme, the New Rule provides that a trustee's compensation must be "reasonable." The Prudent Investor Rule does not suggest a reasonable fee level, but it does direct that a trustee must control the costs borne by a trust. Theoretically, a trustee performs all fiduciary functions personally, and the state statutory rules of trustee compensation are based on the full scope of those functions. Most modern trust documents authorize a trustee to engage investment advisors, attorneys, tax accountants, custodians, and other agents, and to charge their fees to the trust. However, the authority to charge the trust does not necessarily justify it, especially if the trustee is otherwise being fully compensated. If a trustee permits a trust to incur unreasonable costs, he can be made personally liable for the excessive charges to the trust.

Thus one should determine to what degree costs will be deemed prudent by a court. One can find out what other trustees in the community are charging and be guided by those costs. Their reasonableness will depend on the trust's size and complexity, the number of beneficiaries, the number of cotrustees, whether there is a corporate cotrustee, what duties the trustee delegates to outsiders, and how active a trustee must be in exercising discretionary powers.

As a rule of thumb, it would seem that when no corporate fiduciary is involved as a cotrustee and there is no delegation by the private trustee, state statutory fee rates are reasonable. Where, however, there is a corporate cotrustee, or a trustee delegates most of the fiduciary functions, the total of all fees should not greatly exceed a single trustee's fee. In such cases the private trustee might well be advised to reduce his fee. A New Jersey statute requires such a reduction, and other states will probably follow suit. A pileup of accumulated fees can burden smaller trusts, and courts will probably be sympathetic to beneficiaries who complain.

"Reasonable" total fees for a half-million-dollar private trust, combining the trustee, investment manager, custodian, and tax preparer, might total between 1.50 and 2 percent, at today's industry levels, but one should not exceed the standard of one's community, particularly if one uses mutual funds or brokers' "free" custody services.

The settlor can authorize a larger total cost in the trust instrument. However, considering that today's investment management fees hover at the 1 percent level, it is doubtful that doubling that figure will be considered reasonable by the courts, even for the extra services provided.

Trustees and the IRS

A trust pays income taxes like anyone else, with certain exceptions. Depending on the terms of the trust or state law, its cash dividends, bond interest, rents, and other ordinary income are taxed to the beneficiaries if paid to them, or to the trust if the income is accumulated.

A trustee files an income tax return every year (Form 1041). He computes the trust's distributable net income (commonly referred to as DNI), which generally is the trust's gross income receipts less certain authorized deductions, such as a portion of paid trustee's commissions. The trust's net DNI that is actually distributed to the beneficiaries is reported by them on their personal income tax returns. DNI that is accumulated by the trust is taxed to it, and the tax is paid by the trustee when the trust's Form 1041 is filed, on or before April 15 for the previous calendar tax year.

A trust also has capital gains and losses like individual taxpayers. Most often, net realized capital gains are retained in the principal account of the trust under the terms of the trust or state law. Occasionally, they are paid out to a beneficiary, usually under a discretionary power of the trustee. At times a beneficiary will have a power to withdraw principal of the trust. The net capital gains realized in that year will then be taxed to that beneficiary, in proportion to the amount or percentage of trust principal that the beneficiary is allowed to withdraw, whether or not he actually does so. In other words, the *power* to withdraw determines the taxability. In a living revocable trust, since the settlor can revoke the entire trust at any time, all net capital gains realized by the trust in any year are taxed to the settlor, whether withdrawn or left in the trust. Many states also tax any trust income that is not paid out to the beneficiaries.

As a general rule, a trust will not be required to pay estate, gift, or generation-skipping taxes. These are known as transfer taxes, and in our system of taxation the transferor (the decedent, donor, or settlor) incurs the tax and is obligated to pay it. Thus in almost all cases, the donor or the decedent's estate takes care of paying transfer taxes on gifts and bequests, whether outright or placed in trust.

In some situations, however, the Internal Revenue Code makes a trust responsible for the payment of an estate, gift, or generation-skipping tax on assets it receives; the trustee may be obligated to pay the tax. He, of course, can use the trust property to make such tax payments.

A trustee must be aware that if a trust is fully distributed and it turns out that the trust is obligated to pay a transfer tax, he may be personally liable to pay the tax if because of his actions the trust fund no longer has the sufficient funds.

The most common instance of when a trust may have to pay federal estate taxes is in a marital deduction trust. Upon the death of the surviving spouse beneficiary of a marital trust, the trust is taxable in that spouse's taxable estate. The estate tax will be payable either by the surviving spouse's estate or by the marital trust, depending on one of four factors: the estate tax apportionment clause in the will of the first spouse to die; or a similar clause in the surviving spouse's will; or under state law; or (absent all three), by the Internal Revenue Code.

Some states also have estate, gift, and generation-skipping taxes that may apply to a trust and that may expose a trustee to personal liability if not paid. Accordingly, when distributing a trust, the trustee may want to obtain an agreement from the beneficiaries that provides for refunding to the trustee such part of their respective distributions as may be necessary to pay taxes and expenses of the trust that are later determined to be due.

Proxies

A trustee has the power to vote shares of stock held in the trust, unless the trust instrument provides otherwise. Since it can be argued that the failure to vote is potentially detrimental to the interests of the beneficiaries, voting can be regarded as one of the trustee's duties. Of course, a trustee must never vote shares of stock to the detriment of the beneficiaries' interests, or for his own benefit.

A trustee may delegate the power to vote by naming a proxy, so long as he is sure the proxy will not vote the shares against the interests of the trust beneficiaries.

Use of a bank or broker nominee registration allows the nominee to vote the shares of stock unless a trustee specifically retains that power. He is permitted to delegate the power provided it is not used to the detriment of the beneficiaries. A bank or broker will usually vote on investment considerations: preserving and enhancing the value of the underlying shares. This has been called the "Wall Street rule," in distinction from social, political, or religious purposes.

It is important to note that the New Rule's power to delegate a trustee's investment responsibilities does not automatically subsume the power to vote the underlying securities in the investment account. That is a separate consideration, to be defined in each account relationship as it is established. The trustee's choices are as follows:

- To give complete discretion to vote the shares to the investment advisor

- To retain the power to vote all shares of stock held in the account, with proxy forms sent to the trustee

- To specify certain holdings to be voted by the trustee, with discretion to vote the balance of holdings left to the advisor

The last choice is not apt to be made if the trust holds shares in a family corporation or if those shares represent a swing vote or their sale is in some way restricted. Some trusts will hold securities that are restricted either by the securities laws or by a shareholders' agreement, or are restricted by an option plan. The first concern is to not violate any legal or private impediment on the sale. A mistake could expose the trustee to personal liability. Trust records should flag such restrictions.

Investing Under the New Rule

Diversification

The New Rule requires diversification, which has always been considered good policy by trustees. The Old Rule merely encouraged it. This requirement goes hand in hand with the New Rule's reversal of the Old Rule's idea that every holding in a portfolio must be separately examined, or stand on its own bottom, as Harvard likes to say. The New Rule says that only the portfolio *as a whole* must be prudent.

So how much diversification is necessary? We suspect that the answer is, enough to spread risk, so as to avoid large losses. This is often less than one might think.

In the old days, even large companies were often exposed to single industrial areas: A slowdown in domestic appliances could hit General Electric; troubles in the explosives business could hurt Du Pont. These days, however, large companies often spread over many industries. Some single companies are larger than whole foreign stock exchanges. Who can say what 3M makes? The ultimate answer is that this huge enterprise makes no one thing; it makes money. Similarly, today General Electric has an enormous product range. Its largest segment, recently representing 42 percent of profits, is banking! Few investors can name any very large American company that is not multiline and multinational. Thus, today's shareholder of a giant company receives exposure to a variety of both domestic and foreign industries.

Many academic studies have indicated that beyond twenty companies in several industries, little is gained by further diversification; besides, there is an obvious loss in dilution of attention. For the average personal trust, twenty major holdings in several industries would be a fine mix. In practice, one ends up with more and more holdings the longer the trust exists, since it is often good practice to sell some but not all of a very successful investment to find money for a holding in an important new growth sector. Thus, there may be ten large concepts and many more somewhat obsolete but still satisfactory ones.

Obviously, including some mutual funds of different types in the portfolio greatly increases diversification. And some investment categories are best held through funds, such as emerging markets, very small companies, and smaller high-technology companies. Table 4.1 shows some historical correlations between different markets and categories. Some are quite interesting, such as that "large growth" and "large value" march pretty well hand in hand, while "real estate" goes its own way.

Need a trustee invest in foreign stocks for their own sake? Our answer would be that he need not, although he may wish to. The following is a list of some great American companies with their percentages of foreign earnings as of this writing:

Company	Foreign Earnings (%)
AIG	53
Coca-Cola	82
Gillette	63
Intel	58
Microsoft	37
Pfizer	49

TABLE 4.1

SOME CORRELATIONS BETWEEN ASSET CLASSES

Category	Correlation
Large-cap value and small-cap value	Medium
Large-cap growth and large-cap value	High
Large-cap growth and small-cap growth	Medium
Foreign stocks and major domestic categories	Medium
Emerging markets and all domestic categories	Low
Emerging markets and Europe	Medium
Emerging markets and Japan	Minimal
Technology and major domestic categories	Medium
Technology and utilities	Minimal
Technology and all foreign categories	Low
Real estate and technology	Minimal
Real estate and all other categories	Low
Financial and large-cap growth	High
Financial and large-cap value	High
Financial and other domestic categories	Medium
Financial and Europe generally	Low
Japan and foreign generally	Medium
Japan and domestic natural resources, technology and small-cap growth	Low
Japan and all other domestic categories	Minimal
Japan and emerging markets	Minimal
Europe generally and domestic technology, financial and real estate	Low

Notes: Stocks or funds in categories with low correlations—for example, financial stocks and European stocks, or emerging markets and almost anything else—give better diversification than, for instance, large-cap growth stocks and large-cap value. As markets fluctuate, the correlations change, so these relationships cannot be stated precisely.

Source: Adapted from Morningstar calculations, published in the *Wall Street Journal*, with significant modifications.

It is apparent that these companies offer excellent exposure to non-U.S. economies. So the effect of investing in a foreign soft drink or razor blade company is often just to own a less desirable asset, although perhaps more attractively priced, than its American counterpart. At one time foreign stocks tended to be significantly cheaper in price-earnings terms than U.S. stocks. In general, this is less true today, except in countries that are to some degree in trouble. Furthermore, one has difficulty finding great growth stocks abroad, like those just cited, particularly in Europe, although there are some in Japan. Even there, though, the amount of absolutely certain information is often less than one would like. As to value investing, it does not help that a stock seems cheap if one is not certain of all the facts. To our mind the best reason to own a foreign stock would be if the company made something that could not be found here, or if the investor was confident that it was of equally high quality but much cheaper than an equivalent American company. Most foreign markets have been less attractive than the U.S. market in recent years, anyway (see Figure 4.1). And remember, *the United States is the country most friendly to shareholder interests.* Abroad, the shareholder is usually well down the totem pole.

Another diversification question is whether one should own a variety of asset classes. As to the obvious ones, equities, bonds, and real estate (often through *real estate investment trusts [REITs]*), we would say definitely yes, including the latter, assuming that they are attractively priced. Often, however, they aren't, since with money coming in, REIT managements are tempted to overpay for properties. But how about the others? We answer that if a given asset class (e.g., commodities or derivatives) does not offer *an intrinsic buildup in value* based on underlying earnings, then there is a prima facie assumption that it is *not* satisfactory for trust investment. An extremely sophisticated institution may be able to make money in exotica, including derivatives, which may be appropriate for hedging, but in a high proportion of all cases the investor will lose money, sometimes a great deal of money. A number of major banks, and indeed at least one foreign central bank, have lost *all* their capital through derivative speculation.

Need a trustee seek diversification into currencies other than his own? Except for the situation of a trust beneficiary residing abroad, for whom it may well make sense to own some assets in the country in question, we would say no. As to equities, it is not all bad if a currency declines a certain amount, particularly for an exporting company. To some extent one can say that a currency devaluation for an exporting company amounts to a unilateral wage reduction: the sales revenues will be much the same, whereas the local costs, notably labor bills, will be at least temporarily lower, so profit margins should improve. That, of course, is why countries are tempted to devalue.

As to bonds, investors often think that it is useful to invest in a strong currency. However, the interest rate in any currency usually represents the market's judgment at the moment as to the risk of devaluation. In other

FIGURE 4.1

DOMESTIC AND FOREIGN STOCK RETURNS

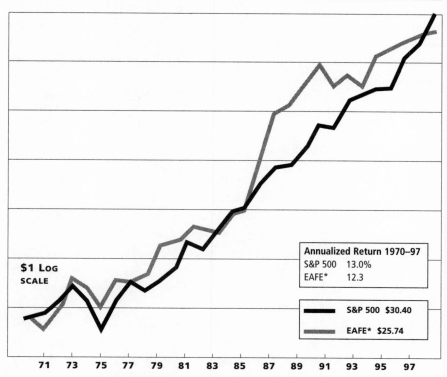

*Europe Australasia Far East index. GDP-weighted with currencies unhedged, in U.S. $.
Source: Reprinted with permission from Sanford C. Bernstein & Co., Inc. From *Investment Planning in the Global Era*, 1998.

words, a bond denominated in a weak currency is likely to bear a higher interest rate than one denominated in a strong currency, and thus it could be just as profitable. For instance, Mexican 91-day peso "Cete" bills have returned substantially more in U.S. dollar terms from their first issue in 1978 through 1997.[1]

So as to both of these categories—equities and currencies—we see no obligation in the name of prudence for a trustee to seek foreign exposure just because it is foreign.

Mutual funds are reasonable trustee investments. One need not, however, diversify extensively among funds. Four to six funds, representing different strategies, such as domestic growth, domestic value, emerging markets, small companies, and fixed income, should suffice. Ten seems like the most one needs for diversification and the most one would in practice follow closely.

It sometimes comes about that for historical reasons a portfolio is overconcentrated in a single company or industry. This does create a prima facie assumption, but not an invariable conclusion, that the trustees should diversify out of that concentration. A frequent and obvious example, control of a family company, can represent a significant value that perhaps should not be sold solely for diversification's sake.

Investing Versus Gambling

Our own views can be summed up by this maxim: A trustee can invest in many things, but he should not gamble.

What is gambling? We contend that it is buying an asset *without an inherent, ascertainable underlying buildup of value* through earnings or interest. Examples would be art or "collectibles." Another form of gambling is buying an asset that may possess this buildup of value characteristic but where neither the trustee nor his agent *has performed enough due diligence to understand it fully.*

Commodities do not offer an inherent buildup of value, and thus commodity speculation is gambling. A commodity broker is running a casino for his own benefit, not working to enrich the customer. Speculation in art is discussed later.

---

[1]Timothy Heyman, *Inversion en la Globalizacíon.* Mexico, Editorial Milano, 1998.

We must recognize that, like the Ford Foundation's highly influential report on educational institution investing policy, which came at the top of a bull market, the widespread passage of the Model Act is also occurring in an environment of high optimism. In Wall Street, doctrine usually follows the course of the market.[2]

Risk

The New Rule, along with the Old Rule and, indeed, common sense, requires that a trustee give due weight to risk factors in choosing investments. In everyday life most of us know what risk is. But in recent years institutional and academic investment theorists have generally equated risk with market price volatility or, in *Modern Portfolio Theory (MPT), beta*. To our mind this is a pernicious conception. A *business* may be extremely stable, and yet its stock may fluctuate. For a true investor, who knows the value of what he owns, volatility can be an advantage, permitting him to add to his holdings when the market is too low and, if he wants, to cut back when it is too high. Would you refuse to buy a house that suited your family because the price had been much higher some years previously? If risk equals volatility, then several years of steadily higher prices in the face of uninteresting earnings might not be considered risky, even though the stock prices toward the end of the period had become grossly excessive. The authors of the highly influential Ford Foundation report on the investment policies of educational institutions were influenced by the prevailing notion that stocks could for long periods rise faster than their underlying earnings. The Ford Foundation ate its own cooking, so to speak, and suffered cruelly as a result; indeed, it had to cut out a third of its programs. Quite often such steady market rises derive from pure momentum. For instance, shares of a closed-end fund in a popular industry may steadily advance to twice the value of the underlying securities. On the beta theory of risk, the shares of the fund would

---

[2] The sardonic but experienced *Grant's Interest Rate Observer*, discussing the Act, writes: "Like an overdressed guest at a dinner party, finance has been encouraged to unbutton its shirt and take off its necktie. What we expect, following the next bear market . . . is that ritualized, rigid, legalistic caution will make its return. In the circumstances that will then prevail, we predict, the change will seem just and reasonable."

then be a low-risk investment, whereas common sense indicates an exceedingly high risk.[3]

The two prices one pays for owning high-growth stocks are low yield, since the company is reinvesting its cash flow in order to build, and market volatility. If one wants to hold growth stocks and nevertheless reduce interim volatility fluctuations, one can indeed hedge against that possibility. But the more one hedges, the more one reduces total return. One is reducing the wonderful long-term advantage of growth stocks and drifting into a fixed-income type of portfolio—much less profitable. Indeed, we have observed that sometimes the most successful portfolios are among the most volatile.

Volatility can indeed become an investment risk factor when there is a mismatch between the maturity of a fixed-income holding and what might happen during the period. If one needs to put aside a considerable sum to pay for a young person's next tuition payment, or for estate or other taxes at a particular time in the future, the common wisdom of the investment business is to buy high-grade debt securities of a similar maturity, so that one can be sure the money will be there when needed. If one buys equities instead, and the market has fallen when one needs the money, it can be both embarrassing and imprudent.

Another authentic risk arises if an older trust beneficiary is living on a program of fixed withdrawals from a balanced portfolio and the trust gets into a position where a sharp market drop, although temporary, could mean that these withdrawals might constitute an inordinately high percentage of the portfolio.

What, then, are the more significant *real* risk elements to which a trustee must give keen attention? Let us note four: business risk, country risk, market risk, and inflation.

---

[3] One hears a bit less these days about another academic favorite, the Efficient Market Hypothesis, which as usually recited holds that since all information about securities is available to everybody, the market always prices securities correctly or "efficiently." The practical refutation of this notion is simply that some investors consistently outperform the market, and some objective measures, such as closed-end fund premiums and discounts to net asset value, fluctuate wildly over time. The theoretical refutation is that (1) *emotion*, along with reason, rules markets; (2) nobody can collect and interpret all possible information; (3) there are different skill levels in investing, as in chess; and (4) when investors do agree on the positive facts about a great company, the stock becomes overpriced: doubts and fears create opportunity. We offer in return the Efficient Professor Hypothesis: All the profs have access to the same information, so all must agree on all matters. Actually, Warren Buffett has intimated that his followers might like to endow a chair in Efficient Market Theory so that he can obtain more investment opportunities.

The first real risk is always the soundness of the business in which the trust is investing. Companies can fail to grow, or indeed can decline, and thus a trustee—perhaps through his advisor—must be aware of shrinking profit margins, declining sales (unit sales as well as sales measured in dollars), skimpy research and development investment, new competition, and so on. This is particularly true during a bull market, when a company's business may be losing ground while its stock price remains strong. Bull and bear markets are like love affairs: When the market is rising, everything is forgiven; when the next bear market comes along, any fault is a ground for rejection.

When a trust holds foreign securities, another true risk is that a country will get into trouble. Its economic environment may be unsound before its security markets reflect that. The impending economic collapses in many Asian countries in 1997–98 were generally not anticipated by the securities markets. (Conversely, of course, things may be better than the market believes.)

Market risk is simply paying too much for a stock, so that the price goes down even though the business remains satisfactory. This can arise from two main causes: The pricing level of the market overall may have become excessive, so that a decline follows; or, without that happening, an investor may still have paid too much for a particular security to which he was attracted.

We have all experienced inflation, which in two generations wiped out much of the value of bonds, insurance policies, and annuities. The New Rule rightly requires that a trustee take inflation carefully into account, as is discussed in the next section.

These, then, are risks that may involve a real impairment of value. Mere quotational fluctuations against a background of improving company conditions need concern a trustee little, as long as the trust in question has a long-term viewpoint.

Inflation and Deflation

Here is a little parable published in his *Forbes* column by coauthor John Train in 1979, when inflation was serious and the Old Rule still governed:

A widow was left a substantial amount of money by her husband when he died. The income went to her for life, with the capital to be divided among their three children after her death.

Her late husband had been a successful New York businessman, and the family had two large houses: one in Greenwich, Conn., and one on Cape Cod, where they went in summer. The children liked coming to the Greenwich place on weekends and spending long periods on Cape Cod in summer, so she kept both. As a result, the widow found herself living at the limit of her resources.

At her annual meetings with her trustees, the problem was aired frankly. How could she maintain the houses and keep up roughly the same standard of living as before, with her husband's considerable salary no longer available? Each year it was decided to sell some growth stocks with low yields and move into bonds or high-yielding equities to maintain the needed income, and hope that all would be well.

So the trust portfolio eventually became roughly half fixed-income securities and half high-dividend stocks, notably utilities and the like.

Unfortunately, however, the investment objective was impossible on its face. At a time when costs are rising 10% a year, income has to rise 12% to 15%, as the tax bracket rises, in order to stay even in real terms.

Now, very few income stocks increase their dividends at anything like 15% a year; and, of course, bond payments don't increase at all.

After some ten years of a princely existence, the widow's buying power in real terms was about 40% of what it had been just after her husband died. The old trustees, friends of her husband, stepped down, and new ones with a more austere and realistic attitude came in. They were dismayed at what they saw. She had to sell both her houses and move into a smaller one, where it was a strain to have any of her children for weekends, since they now had families of their own and came in groups of four or five.

She has many years of life ahead of her, which she will spend in straitened circumstances. If she had cut back right away and adopted a realistic investment policy, she could have been comfortable for her lifetime.

Furthermore, in the future, when the grandchildren come into their inheritance, they will have a justifiable complaint against the old trustees, if they're still around. They can't make out a case at law, but it seems to me that they can certainly make one in common sense and morality. By investing flat out for income at a time of hyperinflation, the trustees knowingly dissipated the corpus of the testator's estate, and thus did violence to his stated wishes and gypped the remaindermen. When the grandchildren ask what happened to their inheritance, their elders will have to explain that it was essentially blown on high living. In fact, the widow herself also has a valid complaint. The original trustees, old business friends of her husband, were paid to give her the benefit of their realism and experience. Why didn't they look ahead and set her on a sustainable course?

This quandary afflicts most trustees of generation-skipping trusts today.

The New Rule, on the contrary, rightly requires specifically that trustees take note of the likelihood of inflation (or deflation). Obviously, extremely few trustees are in a position to do that; even the chairman of the Federal Reserve often gets it wrong. Learned discussions in specialized publications give almost no useful advice. Almost no one foresaw the drastic decline in inflation between 1980 and 1998! The best observation we can offer is that in general, democratic governments have a tendency toward inflation, so this likelihood should always be taken into account when comparing long-term indicated stock and bond returns. By the end of the process described in the *Forbes* column, the remaindermen had been legally gypped, but they had no recourse. Under the New Rule they do, because the trustee must consider the risk of long-term inflation. But for the trustee or investment manager to try to guess the short- or even medium-term direction of inflation and its impact on markets will ordinarily not improve matters.

That said, when the Fed first starts "leaning against the wind" by raising interest rates after the economy shows signs of overheating, one should assume that the process will go on and on in little steps until the Fed has achieved what it desires. The Fed does not leap this way and that; like a glacier, it pushes inexorably until it gets its way. In that higher yield environment, existing bonds will probably decline, particularly long-term bonds. So when one is convinced that the move is real, one should favor the shorter end of the maturity spectrum. The opposite happens when the Fed eases interest rates in a recession: Long-term bonds will probably rise in market value and thus should be favored.

It has long been known that economics is not in general a science in the sense of being predictive, even though banks and other institutions have economists on their staffs. Economics resembles astrology: Quite serious magazines publish astrology columns on which the readers are invited to base their actions for the ensuing period. Many societies have used fortune-telling methods to determine important activities, from when the army should launch an attack to when to start a feast. And yet the same methods have rarely been found useful by later societies. Why do we think economics is different? Perhaps because we live in an age of scientific discovery rather than traditional wisdom, and so are inclined to trust figures—often excessively. The reason economic predictions are rarely successful may be that standard classical or linear economics assumes that there are rational or "clearing" prices for things and that these prices will prevail. Complexity theory and everyday psychology, however, tell us that price movements, being self-reinforcing, usually overshoot both up and down; an asset—including a stock—may sell only occasionally for its theoretically correct price. Anyway, economists' predictions regarding inflation rates will probably be derived from too few variables, incorrectly weighted, and indeed be based on groupthink.

Thus the best single way for a trustee to incorporate inflation or disinflation risk in his investment policy may be to avoid taking extreme positions, remembering that all human affairs are cyclical and that trends do not continue forever.

Here, in any event, is a sketch of investment categories (not necessarily all desirable for a trustee) that should have an advantage under various conditions of more and less inflation:

	Inflation	**Disinflation**
Boom	Real estate, art, "hard" assets	Stocks
Recession	Short-term bonds	Long-term bonds

Incidentally, the *inflation-adjusted* average annual total return figures for various categories of securities illustrate the devastating effect of inflation even more dramatically than the basic figures. The fifty-year comparison is as follows: Common stocks, 7.36 percent per annum; long-term government bonds, 1.90 percent; long-term corporate bonds, 2.44 percent; intermediate-term government bonds, 2.02 percent; U.S. Treasury bills, 0.60 percent. (A thirty-year calculation is shown in Figure 4.2.) If one further applies the impact of taxation, which falls relatively lightly on long-term growth stocks, the disparity is even more striking, as shown in Figure 4.3.

Sources of Information

A Trustee's Information Sources

This book is not a "how-to" investment guide, and most of what we have to say about information sources will thus be cautionary. Our first observation

FIGURE 4.2

AFTER-TAX AVERAGE ANNUAL RATES OF RETURN

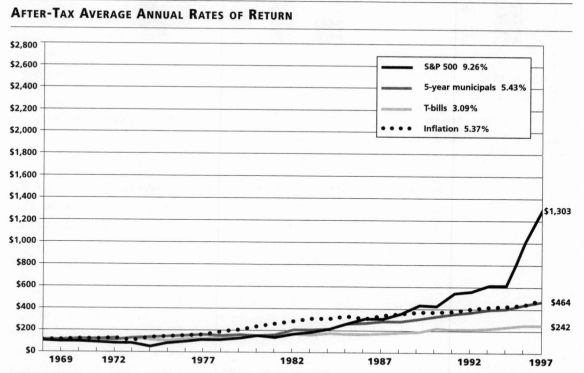

Maximum applicable federal income and capital gains tax rates applied 1969–97, 24 percent capital gains tax applied in 1997. 33 percent turnover for stocks and 10 percent turnover for bonds.

Source: Reprinted with permission from Brown Brothers Harriman & Co.

FIGURE 4.3

THE EFFECT OF TAXES AND INFLATION ON TOTAL RETURN (1926–98)

ANNUALIZED RETURNS*

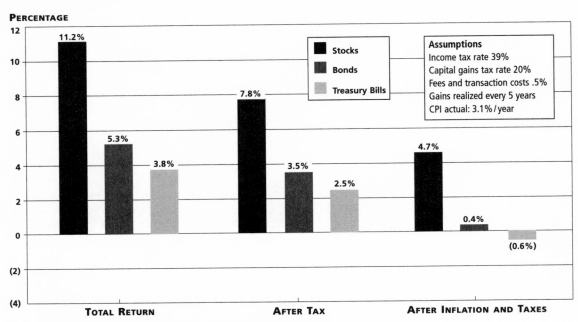

*Adjusted for taxes, fees, and inflation (1926–1998). Stocks = S&P 500, bonds = long-term government bonds.
Source: U.S. Trust Corporation.

is that one should avoid a short-term point of view or short-term advice. We know trustees who worry about short- and medium-term market movements, but since trusts intrinsically have long-term objectives, and since short-term movements are unpredictable anyway, this is a waste of time. When successful equity investing means holding a few excellent stocks for extended periods, getting to know them better and better, why cope with hundreds of new ideas a year?

What does work is identifying excellent growth stocks that are not overpriced, and that one can hope to hold for a long time. A convenient way to do this is to "reverse engineer" major holdings of outstandingly well run mutual funds or investment management firms. A book[4] by one of the present authors describes this approach.

[4]John Train, *The Craft of Investing* (New York, HarperCollins, 1997).

Finding valid investment ideas can challenge an individual trustee. One needs to generate reliable facts and ignore tips. Almost all professional investors find the Value Line Investment Survey extremely useful, although its rankings should not be relied on. The top-ranked stocks do better than the bottom-ranked stocks, but the Value Line funds, which follow this system, have mediocre performances, perhaps because of transactional costs. A trustee should read *Fortune* and *Forbes* and may find *Business Week* helpful.

The *Forbes* annual mutual fund survey is the most satisfactory source of statistical information on funds. Most such surveys in other publications are simplistic. *Forbes* rates their performance in both up markets and down markets, although since markets tend to rise over the long term, the "up" component should receive the most attention.

There seem to be surprisingly few really helpful investment books. Most serious practitioners read *The Intelligent Investor*, by Benjamin Graham, a wise work, written, however, before the era of high-technology growth that we have entered. We find much good sense in *The Only Other Investment Guide You'll Ever Need*, by Andrew Tobias (Bantam Books).

Market Letters

All too many trustees invest their trusts according to the advice found in one or several market advisory letters. We consider this practice to be in general ipso facto imprudent. A trustee should not base his actions on market letters. It seems to be a general truth that the best-known ones deliver the worst performances. The most famous market letter swami is Joe Granville. A flamboyant showman, he is one of the handful whose pronouncements have themselves moved markets. A notable instance occurred on January 6, 1981, when the Dow Jones Industrial Average broke 1,000 heading up and Granville trumpeted: "Sell everything!" The press picked up his announcement, and the market promptly fell 24 points—equivalent to a little short of 250 points today. Not bad. That, however, was just at the start of the great Reagan bull market of the 1980s. In December 1995 Granville predicted a Dow Jones crash to 2,350. In fact, the Dow quite soon rose over 10,000. Dropping out was costly.

A useful service called the Hulbert Financial Digest of Alexandria, Virginia, calculates how you would have made out if you had actually followed the advice of these market letters.

In Granville's case, for the five years through 1987, he lost his followers 97 percent of their invested capital, followed by a loss of 94.7 percent through mid-1992. That would leave many investors with little money—or incentive—to continue their subscriptions.

For the five years ending April 1995, Granville lost 83.7 percent, and 96.6 percent for the previous ten years. Put differently, from December 1990 through November, 1997, Granville lost you 28.6 percent of your money a year, compared with a gain of 18.8 percent for the Wilshire 5000 index. After all this, no responsible trustee could reasonably follow Granville's advice, unless—most imprudently—he failed to examine the record.

Another famous prognosticator is James Dines, formerly self-celebrated as the supreme "gold bug" who, unfortunately, made some disastrous calls in that metal. Over the ten years ending in April 1995, *The Dines Letter* lost its followers 8.1 percent a year. Advancing to a more recent period, over the ten years ending November 1997, he lost only 0.4 percent a year—much better, except that the Wilshire 5000 gained 18.8 percent a year over that time.

During the same period, the heavily touted *International Harry Schultz Letter* gained 5.5 percent a year, a bit dull compared with 18.8 percent for the market. That was, however, a benign result compared with the *Overpriced Stock Service*—very overpriced indeed at $495 a year—which delivered a loss of 59.8 percent per annum.

Market advisory letters often obfuscate their own results. The unsuccessful Schultz describes himself as the "most honored" of the fraternity. Hulbert cites *The Option Advisor,* which, after 1983, has delivered its faithful a 2.7 percent annual loss compared with a 15.5 percent gain for the market overall. Yet its advertising maintained sturdily that its "proven" advice "puts 90 percent of the other investment advisories to shame." Alas, over the period, it has in reality outperformed fewer than 10 percent of them.

For that matter, Granville has been wont to advertise that he proclaimed a "buy" signal immediately after the market's jarring 500-point drop in 1987. Deft! But less so when you learn—not from his ads—that he also issued such a signal *before* that drop.

The U.S. Securities and Exchange Commission (SEC) accused Stephen Leeb's market letter, *The Big Picture,* of claiming that his market-timing formula would have transformed $10,000 into $39 million in twelve years. The SEC complained that to achieve this result required applying *retroactively* a number of subsequent changes in the program. So the brilliant result could not, in practice, have been achieved by his readers.

To sum up, only a tiny handful of the market letters deliver consistently superior results. Most have to be trend followers and momentum players. When stocks, or an industry sector, are declining, they urge you to sell. When the market, or a sector, is booming, buy aggressively! But *the problem with momentum investing is that the river rushes most rapidly just before it plunges over the falls.*

Thus, we are confident in asserting that trustees who base their investment decisions on ideas culled from market letters, even many market letters (which does not improve matters), convenient though this course appears, are not exercising care, or skill, or caution.

How about lists culled from investment magazines? Most are to be ignored, but some are interesting. Figure 4.4 shows the result of holding *Fortune's* annual ten "most admired" companies for the subsequent decade. The results were satisfactory but not remarkable. One notices that the companies that were on one list but not the other did better than the ones that were on both.

Technical Analysis

In our opinion, technical analysis does not form a proper basis for investment decisions and should not figure in a trustee's calculations. It is a hopeful shortcut. Mankind craves attractive easy formulas, to avoid hard or painful thought, and people will resist to the death—sometimes literally—facts that could disabuse them of cherished beliefs and pleasant dreams. *A trustee should focus on the study of value.*

As to technical analysis, one should make a distinction: *Market analysis* is a look at how far the pendulum has swung, so to speak, in terms of its traditional range—like taking a patient's temperature. In other words, if industrial stocks are selling near a historically high multiple of their replacement value, then obviously one should take care. If individual

FIGURE 4.4

FORTUNE "MOST ADMIRED" COMPANIES FOR 1987 AND 1988: ANNUALIZED RETURNS IN THE SUBSEQUENT DECADE

1987 LIST

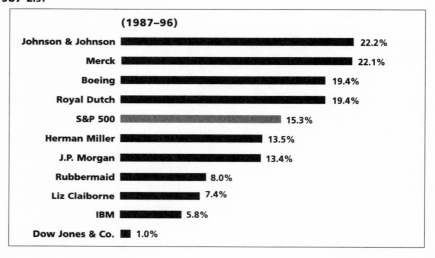

1988 LIST

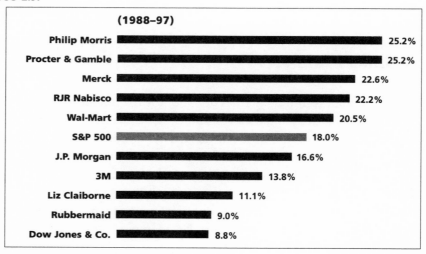

Source: Reprinted with permission from Sanford C. Bernstein & Co., Inc.

stocks are selling for much less than replacement value, or, indeed, less than cash in the bank net of all indebtedness (as happens occasionally), then one stands on solid ground. These simple indices are reasonable and systematic. They should be used not necessarily to predict the future but to give us an idea of where we are. All good investors take general note of these criteria. It is useful to look at the chart of a stock when one is thinking of buying it.

Charting is what does *not* work: reading the patterns of the dotted lines: "rounding bottoms," "head and shoulder tops," "flags," "pennants," and all that. This subject has been studied to death, and has invariably been shown not to yield consistent results for any considerable period. Some firms have spent millions of dollars testing these systems, looking for the philosophers' stone. Usually, after such an investment, the group that has spent the money feels it should offer the service to customers. However, what has been done is called a "playback" or "data mining": One develops a formula that would have done handsomely up until just recently. Alas, it turns out not to work consistently in the future. We have been exposed to literally hundreds of these analyses, some extremely impressive, and that has always been the outcome.

"Relative strength" is a variation of the same approach. It could work, and perhaps in the future it will, but for the moment it doesn't.

Indeed, one very elaborate study done by a top Wall Street firm showed that there was a slight *reverse* correlation of market performance with predicted results: As the market touched off one of these signals, it did the opposite of what was expected, as traders followed the traditional policy, "Buy on the rumor, sell on the news."

An excellent example of technical analysis in practice is commodity trading. This is generally based on technical rather than fundamental analysis, since in gathering facts the speculator cannot hope to match the big traders in "physicals"—the companies that actually buy and sell the goods because they need them for their own production. Hershey and Nestlé, for example, know more than the friendly commodity trader about the goings-on in the Ghana cocoa market. He therefore is often reduced to exhorting his flock to "buy on strength," "sell on weakness," or whatever. And, of course, there is no intrinsic buildup of wealth going on here, just a betting game; the friendly trader, like the casino croupier, is in business to make money for the house, not the customer.

A book by one of the present authors called *The Money Masters* describes the activities of a then highly successful commodity speculator who, before getting rid of all his customers and trading entirely for his own account, had spent his business life as a trader for a number of well-known firms. During this time he had dealt with about a thousand customers. How many of these customers made money over any considerable period? *Not one!* In the commodity business it is accepted that the life of a customer is about six months, by which time he is very likely indeed to have lost all the money he had available to gamble in this way. Our point is that here one has a valid laboratory test of technical analysis, going on every day. It's easy and cheap, but it doesn't work, any more than "systems" in gambling casinos work. A tiny handful of players may succeed, but no more than that.

One is not surprised to find hundreds of tip sheets, market letters, and on-line services offering advice on charting technical analysis of stocks and commodities. Such fortune-tellers exist for all human activities. Even the cookies offered in New York Chinese restaurants include suggested winning lottery numbers. "Tell them what they want to believe" is the first rule of propaganda. However, we find it deplorable that solemn investment books published by reputable houses include chapters on chart-based commodity speculation as though it were a bona fide way of building wealth.

The Pitfalls of Speculation, published near the beginning of the century by Moody's, states: "There is an incredibly large number of traders who pin their faith to the so-called chart system of speculation. . . . The idea is untrustworthy, absolutely fatuous, and highly dangerous." That was in 1906; it will be just as true in 2006 and 2106.

Investment Vehicles

Mutual Funds

Stock mutual funds, if the costs are low, are often a more suitable investment for a trustee than he may realize. They can be an excellent way to achieve diversification. The Morningstar and Value Line services provide useful information on many funds, but the top-ranked funds in both underform the market. (See footnote 7 in this chapter.)

Obviously, a trustee should practically never pay a selling commission or *load,* since he can almost always find as good a fund without such a charge as with one, and *prudence requires controlling costs.* A number of studies have shown that load fund investors have a performance experience comparable to no-load investors in funds of similar orientation. However, this is entirely attributable to the tendency of load fund investors to stay on board longer. If the trustee expects to be able to resist the temptation to jump about, no-load funds offer every advantage. Funds with "12 b-1" fees to cover marketing costs, on the theory that a bigger fund is better, work to the disadvantage of the shareholders. In general, smaller is better.

Incidentally, it is not necessarily a true benefit for a mutual fund to offer its shareholders "switch privileges." The redoubtable Peter Lynch, sometime chief of the Magellan Fund, has stated that while the performance of his fund was brilliant, the results obtained by most of his investors were mediocre. The reason is that most retail investors get excited near the top of a market, or when a sector rises, and buy. At the next drop, they lose heart and switch out again.

That could mean that while the fund goes from 20 to 30, a specific investor could come in at 26 and go out at 24. This phenomenon is masked by the rising net inflow of cash. Thus a cardinal rule is: *Don't trade funds* (or stocks, for that matter).[5]

If it is a bond fund, the trustee should ascertain the investment quality of the instruments, including repurchasing agreements (repos) and other yield-enhancing strategies. In a stock fund, one should look at the portfolio turnover. In general, the higher the turnover, the worse the performance. Broker-run funds often have high turnover. The SEC has found that for each percentage point of increased expense level in a fund, its annual return drops not 1 but 1.9 percentage points, apparently because of the performance penalty of higher turnover. Funds run by

[5] Over the fifteen years from 1982 to 1997 the S&P 500 returned 19 percent a year, while after costs, funds returned 15 percent: still all right. Alas, the average fund *investor* only earned 10 percent a year, because he was trying to be clever. (Greenwich Associates, cited in *Fortune,* December 2, 1998.)

stockbrokers for commissions return about 0.6 percent per year less than those managed for a fee.

One must, of course, understand the quality of the securities held. In a severe market break there may be no buyers at an acceptable price for low-quality stocks. And funds with high turnover saddle their shareholders with constant capital gains taxes for which their performance figures do not adjust.

To be sure, a few satisfactory funds violate all these principles: mutual funds that charge a hefty selling commission, have high turnover, hold low-quality securities, and nevertheless perform well. However, these are anomalies. The trustee has no reason to tempt fate by favoring them.

As to long-term bonds, since they contain far fewer uncertainties than stocks, and since their risk is evaluated by rating services, we would say that in general the trustee should buy them individually, not through funds. Also, there may be repos and other yield-enhancing but risk-increasing maneuvers going on in a bond fund of which the fund holder is unaware, even in government bond funds.

Furthermore, the burden of fees and expenses relative to net return in a bond fund can be heavy. Suppose a gross yield of 6 percent; after tax that might imply a return of 4 percent (and after inflation only 2 percent). A 1 percent expense level means that the beneficiary is giving up a significant part of his true net return to pay for a service that a competent trustee could easily perform himself. Exceptions to this rule could include junk bond funds, which can be worthwhile, and foreign bond funds. Note that some junk bond funds charge much more than others with similar performance. We see no justification for buying a fund with such a fee structure.

As already mentioned, one need not diversify extensively among funds, which are already diversified, particularly if they are in different sectors.

Here are some further mutual fund investment principles. In the first place, a good fund is usually run by an identifiable individual. Ideally, if a trustee proposes to make a large fund investment, it is not a bad idea to try to visit the manager in his lair to apply a few commonsense sniff tests. Top money managers usually have huge amounts of paper on their desks, sometimes measured in inches; when they talk about stocks, their eyes often glitter like those of a hunting dog scenting a game bird. Beware the young enthusiast who has done brilliantly for a while—what one might call the Icarus syndrome. With a distressing frequency, he plunges to earth in the next bear market. His investors will be "hot money," so that the poor manager has to scramble wildly to meet redemptions as the quotations melt away. One should select a veteran campaigner, a manager who has done well in hard times.

Since as we write no one with less than a decade's experience has gone through a real bear market, the young swinger who is familiar only with reaching for hot ideas and pyramiding his profits, and whose income is in direct proportion to his results, can run you onto the rocks.

Then, too, when one studies the spectacular results of a jazzy fund with a view to taking a flyer, be sure to find out if these have been achieved by using derivatives. They are more common as a means of yield enhancement in fixed-income situations, but they also can happen in stock funds—an extremely risky technique. Quite often the prospectus may not tell you.

A phenomenon we have all seen occurs when the star manager of a particular fund bolts the management company stable and starts up on his own. Be cautious about signing up with him right away. The most famous such episode occurred when Gerry Tsai left Fidelity in the 1960s to start up the Manhattan Fund, the largest fund launch to that date. The result was catastrophic. In the words of Alexander Pope, "Be not the first by whom the new is tried / Nor yet the last to cast the old aside."

Often a manager will lose his touch when he goes out on his own. One can understand why. He will have been cosseted by in-house researchers and traders whom he has learned to lean on. If he has been accustomed, say, to the superb backup of a Fidelity, he might stagger for the first year or two after he breaks loose. One often finds a similar loss of bite when one fund group sells out to another. Finally, one should be suspicious of a fund whose star manager has just departed. There are very few star managers, and no worthy replacement may be available.

As already mentioned, one should, in general, avoid a fund with high turnover, usually the enemy of good results.

Be sure that a fund is run by a sponsor of outstanding probity and financial strength. Sometimes things get out of control, with heavy losses. The parent company may step in and rescue the situation, if it is honorable and financially strong. Otherwise, it may just walk away from the situation.

Index Funds

In our opinion there are five merits to buying an index fund—one that seeks to mirror the performance of the S&P 500 or another index—and certain disadvantages.

1. The first merit is that one can achieve ample diversification at a low fee with a small amount of capital, which might otherwise not be possible.

2. The second is that turnover is kept minimal, further reducing costs.

3. The third is that one avoids egregious follies, since one is spared exciting ideas, which have a tendency to burn out promptly.

4. A fourth merit is convenience: one does not get complicated letters from brokers and custodian banks.

5. The fifth is not having to make decisions: indexing is a no-brainer.

These last two virtues might be called the "aspirin function": peace of mind. A valuable merit, unless it lulls one too far. And a trustee is paid to worry.

On the other hand, there are also disadvantages, the most obvious being the cost, which should be low, but often is not.

And the cardinal merit of index funds, namely, gaining diversification, suffers from an offsetting flaw that can be expensive. A trust may achieve wonderful performance by finding a few Great Winners that it lets ride on and on until they dominate the portfolio. One true maxim of good investing is "Let your profits run." In an index fund, and probably not in a mutual fund, that cannot happen.

A particular caution one should remember when using index funds, is that a trustee may fail to choose the strategy appropriate to the trust's particular circumstances. It's as though one wore the same clothes winter and summer. Younger persons should be saving up for their later years, taking advantage of the miraculous growth that compound interest brings about. For such a beneficiary, growth stocks, with high reinvestment rates and taxable low dividend payouts, make excellent sense. For an older beneficiary, however, an income strategy can be attractive, particularly since the older beneficiary's tax rate declines with the end of his peak earning period.

Often, however, buyers of index funds do not bother to choose the most appropriate index to tie on to, arbitrarily opting instead for the S&P 500 or whatever.

Few investors realize to what extent index investing has become momentum investing. In recent years a handful of stocks have moved the S&P 500, and, even more, the NASDAQ Composite Index. In 1998 the top five stocks contributed 25 percent of the S&P 500 performance and 70 percent of the NASDAQ; the top ten stocks contributed 41 percent and 82 percent respectively! (See Tables 4.2 and 4.3). These are not broad cross-sections of American industry, as was the case as recently as 1995, when the top ten in the S&P 500 only contributed 13 percent of the performance. For real diversification today the investor should consider the Russell 2000, which is explained in the Glossary.

To sum up, a diversified and virtually unchanging portfolio of growth stocks for a younger beneficiary, or stocks paying a comfortable income for an older beneficiary, either way with minimal turnover and no fees attached, can be a more efficient solution than a fund indexed to an arbitrary average.

On balance, though, the Third Restatement and its Commentary are positive about mutual funds, and, within funds, index funds offer a particularly attractive solution if appropriately used. Since all index funds with similar objectives perforce deliver similar results, we see no justification for buying any whose costs exceed the minimum available from a respectable source, about .3 percent per annum. The Vanguard series often occupies this position, but competitive factors, given the stern cost strictures of the New Rule, should bring about a clustering of index funds at the low-cost end of the scale.

On the other hand, a static portfolio of growth stocks can have no turnover for years on end, and thus no annual capital gains taxes or transaction costs.

Hedge Funds

Is it appropriate for a prudent trustee to hold a limited partnership interest in a hedge fund (also called an investing limited partnership)? Sometimes, if it's a true hedge fund, but not if it's really a conventional account merely configured as a hedge fund. That arrangement will probably be unnecessarily expensive.

True hedge funds—simultaneously long and short, and often trading rapidly—charge very high fees, and sometimes are worth it. But if the fund is really in essence a more or less conventional managed account, one need not pay more than the going management fee for a mutual fund. Excellent results can be obtained for no more than 1 percent per annum if one has the skill to look for this in a managed account, so to pay many times more for a limited partnership doing much the same thing, and often less tax-efficient, is unreasonable. On the other hand, for the best hedge funds, which perform maneuvers beyond the capacity of most investors, the fee can well be earned.

Some hedge funds run more than the invested capital, since they perform a balancing act on margin. In other words, a fund with $100 million in capital may have $90 million long and simultaneously $70 million short, or $160 million under management in all. (Of course, if a hedge fund is running many times its own capital, it risks serious losses if the market acts in some very surprising way.)

TABLE 4.2

Contribution by Stock to Performance of the S&P 500 in 1998

COMPANY NAME (in order of gross contribution)	Beginning Weight 12/31/97 (%)	Base Return (%)	Gross Contribution (%)	Gross Contribution as a % of Total (%)	Cumulative Contribution (%)
1. Microsoft Corp.	2.1	114.6	2.4	8.3	8.3
2. General Elec. Co.	3.2	41.0	1.3	4.5	12.8
3. Wal Mart Stores Inc.	1.2	107.6	1.2	4.4	17.1
4. Lucent Technologies	0.7	175.9	1.2	4.2	21.3
5. Cisco Sys. Inc.	0.7	149.7	1.1	3.9	25.2
6. Intel Corp.	1.5	69.0	1.1	3.7	28.9
7. International Bus. Ma.	1.3	77.5	1.0	3.5	32.4
8. Dell Computer Corp.	0.4	248.5	0.9	3.1	35.5
9. Pfizer Inc.	1.3	68.9	0.9	3.1	38.5
10. MCI Worldcom Inc.	0.4	137.2	0.8	2.7	41.2

Source: Reprinted with permission from Morgan Stanley Dean Witter Research.

Hedge funds can become dangerous in the latter phases of a bull market, when everything seems destined to go up forever. Instead of prudently hedging, as they should, some managers are attracted by the huge fees available at such moments and simply go long on margin. Hedge fund managers, like rival opera stars, are acutely conscious of each other's performances. As a result of these two influences they may try to squeeze the last few percent of profit out of the market, and thus go over the waterfall when the bear phase comes along.

Avoid a hedge fund that gives a profit participation to the manager that is not suspended while he is catching up with a previous decline. It seems astonishing that if in successive years a fund goes from 50 to 100, back to 50, back to 100, and back to 50, the manager should get 20 percent of the increases each time without deducting the losses—that is, without being required to catch up—and yet for some hedge funds this does happen. Such an arrangement should not be accepted by a prudent trustee.

One must always have a lawyer or other specialist in such matters closely examine the partnership agreement and the historical record of a hedge fund. They may contain surprises.

TABLE 4.3

CONTRIBUTION BY STOCK TO PERFORMANCE OF THE **NASDAQ** IN **1998**

COMPANY NAME (in order of gross contribution)	Beginning Weight (%)	Base Return (%)	Gross Contribution (%)	Gross Contribution as a % of Total (%)	Cumulative Contribution (%)
1. Microsoft Corp.	20.4	114.6	21.5	26.8	26.8
2. Cisco Sys. Inc.	7.4	149.7	10.1	12.6	39.4
3. Intel Corp.	15.1	69.0	9.6	12.0	51.5
4. Dell Computer Corp.	3.6	248.5	8.1	10.1	61.6
5. MCI Worldcom Inc.	3.6	137.2	7.2	9.0	70.6
6. Oracle Systems Corp.	2.9	93.3	2.4	2.9	73.5
7. Sun Microsystems Inc.	2.0	114.7	2.0	2.5	76.1
8. Yahoo Inc.		180.8	1.9	2.3	78.4
9. Tel Com Inc. TCI Grp.	1.9	98.0	1.7	2.1	80.5
10. Amgen	1.9	93.2	1.5	1.9	82.4

Source: Reprinted with permission from Morgan Stanley Dean Witter Research.

Funds of funds, notably of hedge funds, even those offered by the Common Fund and the Investment Fund for Foundations, require a close look. Sometimes the disclosed fee at the top level appears modest, but when one adds the fees down at the specific fund level, the total becomes burdensome. Often trustees do not request the information needed to aggregate all expenses.

Options and Commodities

Some claim that a strategy of writing call options on stocks can enhance yield. This rarely occurs if you take account of opportunity cost. That is, the great long-term winner that otherwise would have gone up and up for years gets called away, and the portfolio sits with the dullards.

Sometimes options can help in a diversification program, and a very few highly professional institutions can trade them profitably, but in general they do not suit normal trust portfolio management.

Art

A few trusts own art. On occasion, art is transferred to a trust by the settlor, with the express intention of transmitting specific pieces of family interest to later generations. In our experience, however, works of art are not in general a satisfactory trust investment from a risk-reward standpoint. They lack earning power and are costly to buy and sell, when, indeed, they can be sold at all. Their valuation is subjective. In sum, they are a speculative football.

Probably all works of art together that are sold for the first time on any given day decline in value, adjusted for inflation, after a century, particularly if one deducts a modest opportunity cost. Eventually they disappear, into dust or the attic.

True, institutional investment portfolios have on occasion speculated in art. The most famous such instance was the British Rail Pension Fund. Its results were unsatisfactory, and the trustees renounced the practice.

Dealers and article writers sometimes describe prodigiously successful art investment results. This is usually what statistics calls "survivorship bias." One does not hear about the much greater number of unsuccessful speculations. A work of art should be owned by a person who loves it (and for that reason probably knows about it), not by a trustee charged with preserving capital in real terms. From a personal investment standpoint, art should be bought out of excess income, not out of funds a family may require for living expenses.

Exchange Funds

It can be highly appropriate for a trustee confronted with an oversized position in one stock—typically a former family company—to tender most or all of it to an exchange fund. These ordinarily require about a $1 million minimum per transaction. Such offerings must be analyzed in full by a highly qualified professional, since they are hard to understand.

Establishing an Investment Program

One can identify the following nine steps in designing and executing an appropriate trust investment program. *All should be fully documented.*

1. *Examine the governing instrument* of the trust for indications of the wishes of the settlor. Determine the applicability of the New Rule and other legal constraints.

2. Completely *understand the needs of the beneficiaries.* If a trust has one or more income beneficiaries and one or more remaindermen, consider the ages and financial needs of both categories, taking note of other available assets.

3. *Analyze the recent management* of the portfolio, including investment philosophy and practice, custody and brokerage arrangements, and the performance records of existing managers.

4. Develop a formal, *written statement of investment objectives,* taking account of circumstances and risk tolerance.

5. Having confirmed that the *delegation* is proper, and whether it should be discretionary or nondiscretionary, and after full analysis of quality and costs, make arrangements with outside managers, custodians, and brokers. Design information flow charts and accounting procedures.

6. *Design a hypothetical new portfolio* and then discuss it with those concerned.

7. After completing steps 1 through 6, *execute transactions.* Follow the initial transactions of a new trust or a series of new relationships particularly carefully!

8. *Monitor,* through reports and meetings, the activity of those to whom the various functions have been confided. Occasionally make adjustments as appropriate, notably "rebalancing" and changing manager allocations.

9. Periodically *reconsider* the entire process.

The following are some further considerations as to the nine phases of the trust investment process.

Understand the Terms of the Trust and the Governing Law

Elsewhere we discuss the problems of establishing the legal aspects of a trust's management. Although a trustee need not be a lawyer—and most are not—he should have a general understanding of the law of trusts, just as he should understand the basics of investing.

Understand the Needs of the Beneficiaries

The trustee should fully understand all written intentions of the settlor as to the investment emphasis of the trust to favor the income beneficiaries as against the remaindermen, or vice versa, and any other written intentions. A trustee should assemble full information on the present and future needs and total assets of each class, to the extent possible. It often happens that an income beneficiary does not need additional income and thus would prefer, as a matter of sensible estate planning, to allow the capital to build at the expense of current income for the eventual benefit of the remaindermen, often his children.

Alternatively, if the beneficiary is an elderly person, income needs may be relatively higher, and the tax burden lower. Since in general long-term growth investment is more profitable than investing for high current income, it can be advantageous for a trust instrument to permit a total payout up to a reasonable level (e.g., 4 percent per annum) from a combination of income and capital.

One should understand the *other* trust and personal holdings of each beneficiary. This is an important aspect of the New Rule. For instance, if a beneficiary is personally a large shareholder of a particular class of enterprise, such as high technology, the trustee should take note.

If practicable, the trustee should do a comprehensive plan of all the present and future assets in the settlor's family, together with the amounts needed for living expenses. He should take account of family real estate and art holdings, and also of eventual expectations through inheritance. It sometimes turns out that thanks to the appreciation of some rural real estate, the older members of a family are better off than they realized. They may sell the house in town and move to the summer place, or sell off some acres in the country.

One must of course establish the residence of each beneficiary for tax purposes, so that only appropriate municipal bonds are held. (In our professional practices we often notice that an income beneficiary has moved, while a sluggish trustee has not changed the composition of the tax-free portfolio to correspond.) Sometimes, when high-bracket beneficiaries of a single trust live in different places, it may be appropriate, if allowable, to consider splitting the trust into as many parts as there are taxable jurisdictions. The same is true if the needs of the beneficiaries are different.

Incidentally, one must establish that municipals are the correct solution for an income beneficiary. Short-term corporates are often more attractive after tax than short-term municipals, particularly for beneficiaries in the lower tax brackets, such as younger persons and retirees.

The trustee should also consider whether the instrument permits such transactions as buying all or part of a residence for those beneficiaries who could gain significantly from such an action. It is often tax-efficient and conformable to the wishes of the settlor for a trust to own a residence occupied by beneficiaries, even though this is unusual in American personal trusts.

If the trust beneficiaries include a tax-exempt institution, the trustee must consider the rate of withdrawal, the long-term needs and prospects of the institution, and related matters. Again, the trustee should determine that other trusts for the same institution are not overbalanced in some particular investment category, which could thus be reduced in the trust he is responsible for.

Analyze the Recent Management of the Portfolio

The trustee should examine the present and historical position of the portfolio. What are the explicit or implicit investment policy guidelines? What are the market and other assumptions on which distributions are being made? For instance, if the payout ratio is 4 percent or less, is that too low? If it is 5 percent or more, is that too high? Will the underlying values of the holdings in the portfolio support such a payout?

A successor trustee should make sure that the trust has no claim against his predecessor or against his predecessor's delegated agents.

Develop a Formal Written Statement of Investment Policy

Although it is not legally required, this document is of the utmost importance for all concerned, since it makes available a clear indication of investment intent, much like a military commander's mission statement. It should be formalized after full study and reflection, written down in clear language, and agreed to by delegees if outside managers are to be used. Failure to create such a formal statement invites a presumption of imprudence, like starting to build a house without a detailed plan.

Some of the components of this investment policy statement would include the following:

1. The investment objectives

2. The practical implications of these objectives, such as low income

3. Specific policy indications regarding appropriate or inappropriate securities, given risk-reward considerations

4. A formal procedure for selecting outside portfolio managers or advisors

5. Specific monitoring steps, with a specified review schedule

6. A tickler for review, rebalancing, and reallocation

In other words, it is not sufficient for a trustee to make investments or appoint investment managers based on his feelings of the moment. An investment program should be based on a well-thought-out plan designed to achieve specific investment targets, consistent with the purposes of the trust.

An example of a Statement of Investment Policy and Objectives is provided in Appendix 11. Every trustee should have one, especially if an outside advisor is engaged.

Make Arrangements with Outside Managers, Custodians, and Brokers

Managers A number of outside managers with different specialties should be considered. For large trusts, a trustee should engage managers who specialize in the particular asset category involved, just as one is well advised to buy pizza in a pizzeria rather than in a fish restaurant. If the size of the portfolio is such that a single outside manager will be satisfactory, then the trustee should determine that such a candidate has the wisdom and research base necessary to execute diversified strategies as they become appropriate (see Appendixes 8 and 9 for sample management questionnaires).

The trustee should also consider whether one or more mutual funds are a better approach than, or a suitable part of, an individually managed portfolio of securities. Often they are, since although a fund may well cost more than a managed account of the same manager, it will usually receive his best attention. Some funds do not cost more than a managed account of the same manager. Closed-end funds can sometimes be bought at an attractive discount. Either way, before buying, pay attention to accumulated capital gains!

Custodians For holding and record keeping of trust assets, several custodians of good repute should be considered and a careful analysis of their charges should be conducted. There are wide differences in quality and cost among custodians. Recommendations from trust lawyers and investment advisors are invaluable. For further discussion of this often neglected subject, see "Selecting a Custodian" later in this chapter.

Brokers The choice of a lead broker or brokers should also be carried out in a systematic way, avoiding any direct or indirect financial interest by any trustee, and holding down commission rates. The custodian and/or manager(s) will play a leading part in this process.

Design an Appropriate Hypothetical Portfolio

Based on the foregoing steps, and taking note of current market valuations, the trustee should develop an appropriate strategy. Here he must be able to determine at any moment which sectors seem to offer the best intrinsic values. Often these will be traditional areas that have been unpopular recently, while the less attractive values will usually be those that have been most popular. If at the time in question the price-earnings ratios are much higher than usual in relation to bond yields, then the trustee should be cautious, particularly regarding high-multiple stocks. Sometimes certain categories of foreign stocks, or stocks in specific industries, are popular or unpopular.

An *arbitrary* comfortable permanent allocation process (e.g., 70 percent stocks and 30 percent bonds) apparently will not, in the opinion of the authors, satisfy the New Rule. The choice should be rationally based. The trustee must, either directly through his own knowledge or indirectly through his retained professional advisors, truly understand the values available in the various categories of securities he chooses.

The trustee should be well informed on all categories of securities that may reasonably be considered for the portfolio. However, this does not include all categories that exist in the market. The authors believe, for instance, that, as noted earlier, speculation in derivative instruments, commodities, and certain other gambling categories without an intrinsic buildup of value is inherently unsatisfactory for a trust, although the New Rule does not say so. As noted, a trustee has no obligation to invest in foreign securities qua foreign securities, since he will probably know less about them than about domestic securities, and most of the great American companies have extensive foreign activities.

The authors do not consider that a trustee has any obligation to seek alternative investments (e.g., ventures, real estate, and *leveraged buyouts [LBOs]*) although these may be appropriate for a sophisticated and knowledgeable trustee and certain large trusts.

Indeed, real estate constitutes an extremely important asset class and should be included in many portfolios, perhaps through a traded security, such as a REIT. As mentioned previously, a house occupied for the long term by a beneficiary can well be an appropriate investment for a trust.

Execute Transactions

Particular care is required to follow the initial transactions, to iron out and debug defects in the system, and to resolve glitches. At this point the choice of the individual "point person" in the custodian will have become important.

Monitor Activity

Just as laws do not enforce themselves, one cannot just write out a policy, put it into practice, and then leave the process to itself. One must hold review sessions according to a regular schedule. Are the outside managers doing what they were hired to do? Is their performance satisfactory against designated benchmarks?

Every year or so one should consider rebalancing the portfolio to correspond to the allocations determined previously.

As described elsewhere, one must establish and maintain an appropriate capital and income accounting system.

Periodically Reconsider the Entire Process

At quite long intervals one should review the entire arrangement, including reallocating between managers and perhaps changing other agents, such as brokers and custodians, or their terms. Such "audits" can examine changes in the agent's systems, competitive standing, investment performance, relative costs, staff turnover, and the like.

Trust Investment Strategies

There are many possible approaches to investing. Experience has taught some trustees to favor a very long-term growth stock orientation for individuals. If a trustee buys the stock of a dull company because it is cheap, he may forget to sell it again, or later may be inhibited by capital gains tax liability, so the stock's slow growth will be a drag on trust performance. There is no such thing as a "one-decision stock," but a growth stock carefully researched and bought can sometimes be held for twenty years or more and be immensely profitable. However, a superior manager can go about the investment process in many other ways. Anything can work if one is good at it; thus an investment firm should favor whichever technique or techniques it is best at. These might include the following:

Growth Investing

1. One tries to buy an excellent company whose growth is not reflected in its market valuation, while avoiding the aging "official" growth stock that commands a high price because of its establishment status but whose best growth was in the past. These days the unappetizing term *GARP (Growth at a Reasonable Price)* is coming into favor. Alternatively, it is more work but can be more profitable to buy *very* high-growth stocks.

2. "Emerging markets"—formerly "developing" countries, formerly "underdeveloped" countries. Many of them are indeed growing fast. This is an area of perennial interest, but it can only be executed by specialists, suggesting a mutual fund approach. A nonprofessional has difficulty moving into a new country when the news is bad, let alone when there is "blood in the streets," and yet that is the best time to act. The category should not constitute a large part of a trust portfolio.

"Value" Investing

1. The "Graham & Dodd" approach to finding cheap stocks emphasizes balance-sheet analysis and low price-earnings ratios. One tries to buy a company for less than a bank would lend on it, and ideally in the old days for less than working capital alone. Growth is unimportant. (It can be argued that growth is itself a value, but for this discussion that is a quibble.) Looking for bargains is the safest technique, and the dullest, but in favorable circumstances and with skillful execution it can be highly profitable. The problem is that you get a onetime

move from bargain price to fair value, but after that growth is slow unless you repeat the operation successfully time after time.

The endless cycle of growth-oriented investing and value-oriented investing is shown in Figure 4.5. When either gets too popular it gives way to the other, now out of favor. Investors should pay attention to this cycle, which can last for many years each time.

2. "Asset" investing, particularly in real estate and the extractive industries, where a company's land, timber, oil, or minerals are worth much more than the market valuation. Patience is required.

3. Takeovers, in which an entire company selling below its intrinsic value is broken up and turned into cash or securities of another

FIGURE 4.5

THE GROWTH-VALUE CYCLE

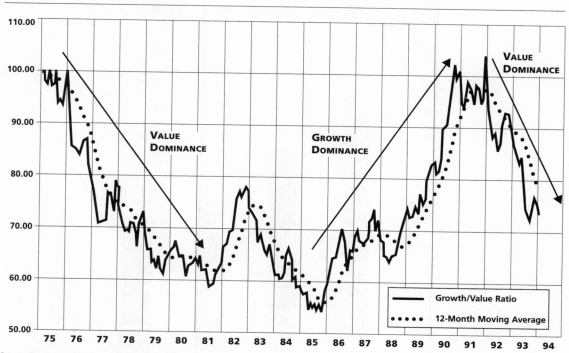

Source: Reprinted with permission from U.S. Trust Corporation.

company. Here one is safest as a member of a group that, if necessary, can actually carry through the takeover.

Trading Philosophies

1. Market timing, trying to buy low and sell high. Unfortunately, if you are in cash at the bottom, you ruin your overall return, as shown in Figure 4.6.

2. Following changing public enthusiasm as it rotates from industrial group to group.

3. Buying particularly depressed issues during a bear market in expectation of a bounce.

FIGURE 4.6

MARKET RETURNS FOR THE DECADE OF THE 1980S

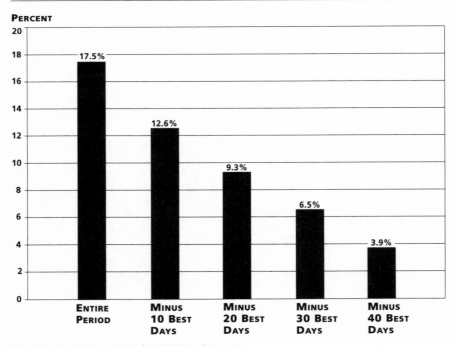

Source: Reprinted with permission from U.S. Trust Corporation.

4. The "Swiss" technique of switching between major national markets, buying the largest and best-known companies in each. The client feels comfortable but doesn't prosper, while the bank collects rich commissions.

Exotica

1. Sometimes the most spectacular technique: investing in small, specialty companies, perhaps with new processes or products in high-growth industries.

2. "Turnarounds": troubled companies where new management is changing things for the better; in general, what Wall Street likes to call "special situations."

3. Hedged investing. One buys an issue that should go up, and shorts one that should go down, hoping to make money regardless of the movements of the general market. Often in the rapture of success hedgers fail to hedge, and one experiences grave losses.

4. Merger (also called risk) arbitrage. Two companies are expected to merge on agreed terms. You buy one stock and sell the other, to make a profit. It's fine unless the merger is canceled, when you lose some money.

5. Speculating in commodities and options. These are gambling games, not investing, set up by brokers to fleece their customers, not to make money for them.[6]

Most of these approaches *can* work out well if done by a specialist. The trading techniques are particularly hard, though, because they are costly in commissions and in the spread between bid and asked prices, so the odds start out unfavorably. They also are keenly competitive. The in-and-out stock trader usually loses money. The disastrous impact of high turnover on portfolio performance is shown in Table 4.4.

---

[6] There are also two legitimate, although highly technical, uses for derivatives: risk control and arbitrage. Even then, counterparty credit status must be of highest quality, or there may be a concealed speculative element to the transaction.

Most managers seeking outstanding performance should focus their attention on an appropriate sector with burning-glass intensity. There is little hope of being superior all over the board. No focus, no superiority.

In practice, trustees have traditionally maintained perhaps 70 percent of a conservative portfolio in superior stocks with strong growth characteristics, and the rest in bonds of good quality in varying maturities. The inherent growth of equities tends to push older portfolios toward a more fully invested position. It then becomes a test of trustee skill to accept some capital gains when the market is euphoric and perhaps repurchase some equities when it is gloomy. We feel, though, that a trustee should not be criticized for declining to attempt market timing, which is usually unsuccessful, in part for the reason indicated in Figure 4.6.

Investment Delegation

Of all the changes made by the New Rule, potentially the most beneficial to private trustees is the power to delegate the trustee's investment respon-

TABLE 4.4

THE EFFECT OF TURNOVER

Manager	Gross Return (%)	Turnover (%)	Return* After Costs and Taxes (%)
A	10	25	7.37
B	10	50	7.06
C	10	100	6.21
D	10	150	5.55
E	10	200	4.70

*Twenty-year horizon.
Assumes that one-quarter of the gains taken at 100 percent turnover are short-term, as are half the gains at 150 percent and all gains at 200 percent.
Portfolio is liquidated after twenty years and all deferred taxes are paid.
Source: Reprinted with permission from Sanford C. Bernstein & Co., Inc.

sibilities for the trust to an outside investment manager. Trustees of trusts situated in states that have not yet adopted the Model Act or a similar law may not be permitted to delegate investment discretion to outside advisors. However, trustees who operate in states that do authorize delegation must be sure that the trust instrument does not prohibit it.

If the trust is governed by the Old Rule, or the governing instrument prohibits delegation, a trustee must make all investment decisions personally, even if he has engaged a professional investment advisor. Such an account relationship is called *nondiscretionary* or *consultative*. The professional gives buy and sell recommendations to the trustee, who decides which to accept. If the advisor acts on his own, even with the trustee's permission, *both* are in violation of the rules and could be held liable for losses.

If delegation is not allowed, the trustee should keep thorough records to demonstrate a nondiscretionary arrangement, including written investment proposals from the advisor, memoranda of meetings or telephone conferences to discuss the proposals, and a record of decisions made.

Some trustees open nominally nondiscretionary investment accounts with an informal understanding that the account manager can really operate on a discretionary basis. The advisor may decide on transactions without first discussing them with the trustee, despite language to the contrary in the account agreement. This temptation is understandable, since individuals often favor discretionary accounts for their own portfolios. But a trustee who tolerates this modus operandi is traveling at his own risk if there are losses.

A trustee who does not have the power to delegate but nevertheless uses an advisor who insists on a discretionary basis is inviting trouble. At the worst, he should require that the advisor communicate frequently in writing about planned investments for the trust, and about details of transactions as they are made. The trustee can then record his ratification of the advisor's actions. This approach may not help defend a liability claim by beneficiaries, but it is better than telling the advisor to do as he likes.

The Model Act provides that a trustee may only "delegate investment and management functions that a prudent trustee of comparable skills could properly delegate under the circumstances," subject to a duty to exercise "care, skill, and caution" in selecting the agent, establishing the scope and terms of the delegation, and monitoring the agent's performance and compliance with the terms of the delegation. The Model Act does not specify how these three requirements should be carried out. We offer suggestions on this subject in other chapters.

Still, after completing the delegation process, the trustee should not heave a sigh of relief and leave matters at that. The essence of sound investment is understanding *value*. In our opinion, even if he hires an outside manager, the trustee should demonstrate care, skill, and caution by understanding broadly what he owns. The trustee needs to learn enough about investing to evaluate his advisors' activities and make reasonable allocations. As to stocks, he should understand the sales, earnings, profit margins, and research expenditures of a cross-section of representative holdings so that he can judge if the whole category seems overpriced. As to bonds, he should understand the relationship of available yield compared with the earnings yields (i.e., the reciprocal of the price-earnings ratio) obtainable from stocks.

And, while the New Rule on its face permits a trustee to do whatever is being done generally, one should remember that from time to time madness becomes widespread. One should be skeptical of the crowd's enthusiasms and fears. The groupthink-prone investor bought growth stocks at fantastic prices in 1973 but by 1974 was likely to sell at much lower prices. So one needs to understand value well enough to bear the discomfort that follows from originality.

The Model Act requires that the trustee develop appropriate strategies, which strongly implies that he should record his reasoning, leaving what we might call an intellectual audit trail. That's fine. We should, however, express a caveat about documentation. Consider what has befallen hospital care. The doctor orders unnecessary tests to protect against malpractice suits; the nurse who once sat at the end of the bed contemplating the patient and establishing a human relationship is now at a desk filling out forms. In fact, a hospital spends an astonishing amount of time on defensive procedures and documentation. This leaves correspondingly less time available for cure. We can only hope that the administrative burden imposed by the Model Act will not curtail the time spent studying the affairs of the beneficiaries and understanding the investments that will enable the trust to prosper.

Selecting an Investment Manager

A trustee should not pick an investment advisor on the strength of hearsay and casual references, or filter candidates based on recent investment performance alone. And any consideration of performance must include down markets as well as rising markets. He must examine more than one firm and carefully analyze each possibility. He must obtain full information on their investment and business approaches, professional resources, financial strength, historical performance, regulatory history and personnel turnover, comparative fees, and other such factors. The trustee must request and carefully study the manager's ADV form, which spells out various details of a registered investment advisor's operation and background; a specimen is attached as Appendix 13. (We are dismayed that so many neglect this essential step.) The trustee should periodically seek updates on all this information.

Institutional investors usually employ a Request for Proposal (RFP) technique to conduct due diligence in selecting managers. A specimen is attached as Appendix 7. Private trustees might do the same, especially for larger trusts.

Appendixes 8 and 9 offer model forms for screening investment managers. Of course, not all trusts need the same breadth of analysis: The forms can be modified according to circumstances. They will also serve as a record of the trustee's prudence in selecting an advisor.

In general, a trustee should seek as much information as possible. Problems arise not when a trustee has done too much but when he has done too little.

Establishing the Scope and Terms of the Delegation

A requirement of the Model Act is that a trustee exercise care, skill, and caution in "establishing the terms of the delegation." What does this mean?

The drafters' comments accompanying the Model Act state that in framing the terms of the delegation, the trustee must "protect the beneficiary." For example, he cannot agree to an exculpation clause in an investment management agreement that leaves the trust without recourse against reckless mismanagement by the advisor; thus he should not automatically accept the standard agreements offered by most investment management firms. He must study the fine print to be sure there are no features that, while permissible in a private relationship, are improper for a trust account. Other potential trouble spots are agreeing to arbitration, thereby waiving recourse to the courts; permitting the broker to lend a trust account's securities; using the advisor's financial products without a fee adjustment to avoid double dipping; failing to invoke the New Rule where appropriate; or permitting a standard of prudence in the account agreement that is lower than the one that the New Rule requires. Appendix 10 offers a form of agreement that should be satisfactory.

So remember: Although the New Rule has lifted most of the old restrictions on trust investing, a trust is still a fiduciary relationship. It exists for the benefit of someone else, and an agent must handle it at a higher level of discretion than he needs for his own money.

Trust funds may be delegated to professional advisors or, occasionally, to stockbrokers. Stockbrokers generally buy and sell securities for commissions, while investment advisors are paid a fee regardless of the number of trades in the account. In general we find it preferable to deal with a professional compensated on a fee basis—which many brokers also do—rather than a commission basis, for obvious reasons. The usual pattern is that the trustee deals with the professional advisor, who then deals with the stockbroker, with whom the trustee need not be in direct contact, although to control costs he should monitor the commission arrangement.

In some countries—formerly in many—a doctor makes his profit on the medicines he sells. But the client or patient is better served if his advisor's income is not linked to the volume of remedies consumed. For this and other reasons, in the English tradition one's legal affairs are looked after by a solicitor who, if necessary, in turn engages a barrister, a specialist who is also a courtroom pleader. Such a separation reduces the risk of a barrister's encouraging a client to litigate. Similarly, the pattern we describe makes it harder for a broker to encourage a customer to trade.

If one does delegate to a broker, whether on a nondiscretionary or discretionary basis, one must be especially careful to arrange for the same sorts of reports one receives from an investment manager, which a broker may not be accustomed to providing.

An investment advisor's fee today usually runs from 0.5 percent to 1.5 percent of the capital per annum, payable quarterly, and is generally tax-deductible. The fee may partially pay for itself in lower brokerage commissions, which are not tax-deductible, since a professional can demand more favorable commission arrangements than an individual, and also in lower turnover, quite aside from the hope of better performance.

An investment management organization has the great advantage, furthermore, of being able to use fully the research and best ideas of many different brokers.

Where, then, do we look for a good portfolio manager, as distinct from a good mutual fund?

One can start by studying the long-term performance figures of the mutual funds in the trustee's home area that are run by investment advisory firms as showpieces and as vehicles for smaller accounts. With some exceptions, a firm's record will usually be shown by the performance of its fund through several market cycles. If you are impressed by one, send for the prospectus and recent reports to see how the performance is achieved. Anyway, when you find a good firm in your area—or somewhere you go regularly—you can visit it. We find that it is more satisfactory to call on the firm than vice versa.

Another way of finding an appropriate manager is, of course, to ask around locally. Here we offer three pieces of advice: (1) Ask about the manager's intellectual honesty as well as his cleverness; (2) seek advice from friends and professionals in related areas, such as trustees and company treasurers, rather than brokers, who have reciprocal arrangements; and (3) identify the individual account manager as well as the firm. A star in a dull firm can often do more for you than a dullard in a top one.

One should interview several firms and try to get to know the person or group that will actually handle the trust portfolio. If the "vibes" aren't right, ask to see somebody else. This is important, because if the investment professional does not inspire the trustee's confidence he will not be able to do his job easily and fluently. He may, in fact, be tempted to deform his policy to accommodate the trustee's own ideas, which may affect the results adversely.

One should not expect to find an arrangement that will last forever. Everything human changes. Indeed, we have suggested that one must keep the relationship under review. In investing, as in any competitive game, an individual or a team may not maintain its relative quality; even if it does, it may get so large and busy that it becomes hard to deal with.

Therefore, one should seek an organization that seems appropriate for the present and the reasonably near-term future, not forever.

Performance

A trustee should study the past investment performance of a possible delegated manager. He needs to go one step further, however.

Often trustees will split the corpus of a large trust into several parts, farm them out to different managers, worry month by month or quarter by quarter about what is going on, and then once or twice a year cut back or fire the worst performers and build up the best ones.

That is too simple.

In the first place, the results will probably reflect the characteristics of the recent market. The growth stocks will have three or four good years, and the growth practitioners will look wonderful. Then those issues will have risen so high they need a rest, so perhaps the low price-earnings issues or the energy or financial stocks have a run, and the specialists in those issues earn the applause. The strength rotates among the various philosophies, and in those periods the manager with that approach looks best.

These vogues usually last a few years, then so many revelers pile on the carousel that it breaks down. Thus jumping from one area where the action is to the next will often result in tying onto the tail end of each fad and participating in one shakeout after another.

The correct approach is to analyze a successful manager's technique for the last five or ten years. If the results have been achieved in a first-class way, then one should ask oneself whether the kind of stocks he specializes in have had a big play recently or whether, on the contrary, they are out of favor and represent outstanding value.

If the latter, then perhaps one has something. Make sure the manager in question is still employing his perennially successful but recently unpopular method, and then hire him. His part of the trust should participate strongly in the recovery that will come along sooner or later. The same manager will probably just have been fired by an overly performance-conscious institution because of two bad years—the same bad years that have coiled the spring for his type of issues to rebound. One can then follow this procedure for as many managers—or mutual funds—as seems appropriate.

It is, incidentally, hard to predict mutual fund performance just on the basis of superior past performance figures, but we believe it is somewhat easier as to managers.[7]

Using an Investment Manager

Obviously, the firm the trustee prefers may not provide superior performance, nor does the Prudent Investor Rule expect that. It should, however, be able to save the trust from expensive blunders and help the trustee develop an investment strategy appropriate to the beneficiaries' situation, on the basis of written investment objectives.

For instance, as discussed previously, the trustee of an older income beneficiary with much more to lose than to gain should direct his investment philosophy toward maintaining the real value of his capital, with reasonable income, rather than seeking maximum growth, particularly if retirement has put the beneficiary in a reasonably low tax bracket.

Often, on the contrary, if the duty of impartiality permits, when a trust beneficiary is comfortably off and in a high tax bracket, one can reasonably invest only for growth, minimizing dividends, and put the beneficiary (if the instrument permits this, as it should) on a "salary," so to speak, of 4 percent or so of his investment assets per annum. The investment advisor is then told to generate that amount in the way that will impose the least tax burden, emphasizing "plowback" stocks. This might result in 2 percent in dividends and interest, and 2 percent in capital growth, for instance. The percentage rate of such a "salary" should take account of market levels, real bond returns, and the like. It should be adjusted every year or two. This requires having written appropriate provisions into the trust instrument.

Properly organizing a client's trust is like designing a house. If the architect executes his job in a workmanlike fashion and employs adequate materials and labor, the house should suit the family that will live in it.

---

[7] The Morningstar five-star category underperforms the market by about 3 percentage points a year, and the *Value Line Mutual Fund Survey* by almost 4 percentage points. The *Forbes* Honor Role Funds do almost as well as the market.

On the other hand, a contractor cannot ordinarily promise to build a much better house than the neighbors' at the same cost. Similarly, an advisor cannot promise that the trust portfolio will outperform the market, only that it will be intelligently designed for the beneficiaries' financial circumstances.

Having agreed with the investment manager on the strategy of the account, the trustee—if the trust instrument and the applicability of the New Rule permit it—should give the manager discretion in executing transactions as long as he stays within the guidelines. If the trustee second-guesses the advisor, the relationship is unlikely to work well. The best stocks often make the beneficiaries uncomfortable because neither they nor the public quite understands them yet. As they become widely understood by investors, they rise.

One should not criticize the manager for short-term adverse fluctuations in stocks that may be bought. Short-term movements—Brownian motion, as it were—are unpredictable and not worth worrying about. The questions to ask are: Is the company prospering? Will it continue to prosper in the future? If the answers continue to be yes, then over time the price will take care of itself.

Rebalancing

If a portfolio falls out of alignment (e.g., the stock-to-bond ratio moves higher than the target) because of success, should one indeed rebalance it? In our view, not automatically. One must consider how the misalignment came about, and whether continuing to hold a winner is not more advantageous than following a formula. Maybe one should change the formula instead. In a very successful individual portfolio, much of the profit will sometimes be made in one, two, or three immensely successful investments that go up and up for years, eventually becoming a large part of the entire portfolio. Since a mutual fund may be steadily taking in new money, which will be added to the holdings and categories that have not advanced beyond the predetermined levels, its great successes thus tend to be leveled off by omission, so to speak. A managed account may prefer to "let its profits run."

A very few investment management firms maintain a high degree of discipline over the various managers. Almost all of the accounts with a given objective and tax status march in step. When Merck goes on the buy list, the manager of every growth account must buy some or produce a valid excuse: for example, too much Pfizer in the account already, no free cash, or whatever. If the firm enjoys a superior stock selection capability, then this arrangement produces the best results, and the best-performing firms are often run this way.

More usual by far, however, is a mediocre stock selection process, which means that there is little reason not to give considerable latitude to each manager within the firm. Almost all brokerage houses fall in this category; such firms allow their reps to recommend more or less what they choose, within reason, unless the firm has developed a specific policy for or against some particular stock or industry group. In dealing with such firms, then, more than ever one needs to find the right executive for the account.

Many beneficiaries—particularly, for some reason, those who are successful in business—are very conscious of losses, even if the gains are outstanding. In such a situation the trustee and manager may feel that the safest strategy, in terms of their own interest, is to invest defensively. The manager should explain to the trustee and the beneficiary that this attitude may affect his performance and should resist the pressure to depart from his best strategy.

As a meeting with an advisor ends, one should then and there schedule the next one. Points requiring study or action always remain, and having a deadline sharpens things up.

Selecting a Custodian

A trustee always looks closely at an investment manager's costs but often looks less closely at a custodian's. He must, however, satisfy himself that the custodian's services are satisfactory and the charges competitive. Typical charges run to less than 40 basis points (0.4%) for a money market account, less than 30 basis points for a small private account, and less than 10 basis points for a very large account. The correct procedure is to lay out the charges and characteristics for various custodians on a grid, including the following:

1. Annual account charges

2. The frequency (which should be daily) and cost of sweeps of dividends and interest into an interest-bearing account

3. The formulas for setting the interest rates on such accounts

4. All other charges, such as check-writing and transaction recording

5. Efficiency

6. Consensus of references

In no event should a trustee sign a margin agreement with a brokerage house that is acting as custodian. Such an agreement risks the securities going into the broker's general assets in the event of its bankruptcy, rather than being segregated.

A prospective customer should talk to a number of other customers of the same custodian and record their comments on its efficiency. One should ask for references and check them: if possible, talk to former customers of the custodian and to present customers not suggested by the custodian.

Different custodians vary greatly in efficiency. In general, a trustee should only deal with one that is highly efficient, and is equipped with the particular account record system needed for trusts, without which life will be miserable. One needs to identify and rate the individual who one will be dealing with within the organization, and who will thus be unscrambling the inevitable glitches.

For Investment Managers

Discretionary and Nondiscretionary Management

A manager who is approached by a trustee to open a *discretionary* investment account must first determine if the trustee really has that authority. This will usually require legal advice, or at least an opinion from the manager's compliance department. If the authority does not exist, notably because the Model Act or a similar law has not been adopted by the trust's state of domicile, or if the instrument is unclear, the safest approach is a nondiscretionary account, where decisions are approved in advance. In accepting a discretionary trust account an investment manager must establish that the trustee has the power to grant it. If the trustee does not have that power, the manager may be liable to the beneficiaries for loss. In addition to verifying a trustee's delegating powers, an investment manager should have a grasp of the general duties of a trustee, especially those bearing on trust investment. Trust accounts are generally run in a different manner from private individual accounts.

Nondiscretionary Accounts

Some trustees prefer a nondiscretionary account arrangement to a fully discretionary one. In such instances the manager probably does not incur fiduciary responsibilities with respect to the trust, although he may have some residual duty to determine if the trustee's directions or approval of the manager's proposals are prudent under the law and consistent with the trust purposes. Discretionary arrangements are clearer. Above all, one should avoid a hybrid account arrangement, where the account is nominally discretionary but actually operated in a nondiscretionary way. Document such arrangements carefully. Decisions often fall between the cracks.

The New Rule provides that investment decisions for a trust *must* be evaluated "not in isolation but in the context of the trust portfolio" and as a part of an "overall investment strategy, which should incorporate risk and return objectives reasonably suited to the trust." The Model Act lists eight factors that may affect the trust or its beneficiaries:

1. General economic conditions

2. The possible effect of inflation or deflation

3. The expected tax consequences of investment decisions or strategies

4. The role that each investment or course of action plays within the overall trust portfolio, which may include financial assets, interests in closely held enterprises, tangible and intangible personal property, and real property

5. The expected total return from income and the appreciation of capital

6. Other resources of the beneficiaries

7. Needs for liquidity, regularity of income, and preservation or appreciation of capital

8. An asset's special relationship or special value, if any, to the purposes of the trust or to one or more of the beneficiaries

The Model Act continues many of the Old Rule's duties, which is why we urge investment managers who will be handling trust accounts—

particularly discretionary ones—to familiarize themselves with the key fiduciary principles governing a trustee's activities. The most important is that a trustee's investment choices must first and foremost suit the *specific purposes* of the trust. Hence, a portfolio of prudent holdings that performs well compared with benchmark indices but falls short in liquidity needs, income levels, or diversification, all permissible for private individuals, may run afoul of the New Rule—and the Old Rule as well.

Investment managers know that the ERISA law covers investment management accounts for qualified employee benefit trusts. ERISA, being a federal statute, applies across state lines. Private trusts are different, and investment managers must determine which law, including state law, governs the investments of each private trust they handle. During the present Model Act transitional period, three possibilities exist: the Old Rule, the New Rule, and the trust, which can override the other two. This determination should be made by legal counsel.

Since the terms of each trust document control, an early order of business for an investment manager is to review the digest of the trust's terms or, if it doesn't exist, to prepare one (see Appendix 2 for a sample digest).

The digest will also convey such important matters as the trust's governing law, which may not be the settlor's domicile; tax information; income objectives; cotrustee and legal counsel identification; remainder provisions; invasion of principal authorization; termination and remainder provisions; and the like. The digest may also indicate whether the duty of impartiality applies or is abrogated and whether there are investment restrictions or mandates.

Although most professional investment managers develop a favorite investment style for all of their accounts, in private trusts a separate, appropriate strategy must be developed for each trust portfolio. Yet experience shows that private trustees rarely do so. To repeat, *every private trust investment account should establish its own portfolio strategy and objectives,* preferably in writing, although that is not a legal obligation (see Appendix 11 for a sample statement).

A private investment trust's manager should start his investment program by analyzing the trust's tolerance for loss and its return expectations. The Model Act treats the liquidity needs and the timing needed to meet a trust's distribution requirements as key responsibilities of a private trustee. Managers familiar with dealing with the liquidity requirements of an ERISA account should have little difficulty in handling this aspect of a private trustee's investment duty.

Alas, since it is so hard to satisfy both the income beneficiaries and the ultimate takers of the trust principal, the duty of impartiality is known in some trust circles as the duty of impossibility. Rarely will both classes be happy.

A few trusts specifically exclude the duty to act impartially as between beneficiaries. The planning theory in such cases is that most trusts have a preferred beneficiary, usually the income beneficiary, and the impartiality rule interferes with the settlor's real intentions.

Sometimes the trustee is also given a broad power to invade trust principal for the preferred beneficiary. This permits greater tax efficiency by seeking capital gains rather than ordinary income, as long as the power is not limited by standard "health, support, and education" guidelines.

A trustee is required by the Model Act to control (not minimize) costs, including investment manager fees. An investment manager should establish that overall outside agent costs are not unreasonable or excessive. They may be examined by a court upon petition of a beneficiary. Courts sometimes force trustees to pay back fees that they deem unreasonable. That could also happen to an investment advisor.

This is not to say that a trust's advisory fee has to be lower than other account fees, or that special fees, such as hedge fund incentive fees, are not permitted. The issue is *reasonableness,* both in absolute terms and compared with competitors. (Some advisors may feel that they are entitled to a higher fee given the burdens imposed by the Model Act!)

Special care is required when other products of the advisors are being used. There should be full disclosure to the trustee and no "double dipping," as when a trust's investment advisor uses its own mutual funds without adjusting its fee.

An investment management agreement should allocate the manager's investment advisory fee as between income and principal. Many states dictate the allocation of fees for trust services, but the trust terms can modify it. Usually, state policy will either charge the income and principal of the trust equally, or allocate a larger percentage to principal, on the reasoning that investment services are directed more to increasing capital than income.

The manager would do well to set out the different available service arrangements in a separate document for discussion during the initial interview, rather than just insist on the set language of his standard account agreement.

Monitoring

Since a trustee who delegates has a duty to monitor the performance of the discretionary manager, it helps if the manager proposes a reporting and meeting procedure to verify that his policies are consistent with the trust's objectives and the needs of the beneficiaries.

Since the authority to delegate to an investment manager is new in private trust law, it can be a good marketing strategy to help the trustee perform his delegation conformably to the New Rule.

Revocable Trusts

Since the settlor of a revocable trust owns the trust property and reserves all beneficial interests, some professional managers wrongly treat it like an individual portfolio. A revocable trust is still a trust, and absent special provisions the trustee, be he the settlor or another, still owes the fiduciary duties imposed by the Model Act to the remaindermen who will take the trust property when the settlor dies.

Terms of the Trust Exception for Private Trusts

Unlike ERISA, the terms of a private trust can eliminate most of the normally applicable conflicts of interest and similar duties of a private trustee under the prudence standard. Such terms of a trust may permit an investment manager to do things that would be prohibited in an ERISA relationship.

Summary

The Model Act offers investment managers a real opportunity, but at a price. It raises the standard of care for a private trustee's managing of a trust's investments, but it lets him delegate to a discretionary agent, who comes close to *being* a fiduciary himself. Investment professionals must understand the increased responsibilities that the new Act imposes, including heightened focus on compliance and costs.

One should bear in mind that the ability to delegate discretionary authority is not in effect in all states as of this writing. In new trusts, and especially revocable ones, it may help to have the terms of the trust explicitly derogate any duty of impartiality, or the Prudent Investor Rule itself, to minimize the exposure of a trust's trustee—and hence, the investment manager. But the one standard that cannot be abrogated is the duty to act with care, skill, and caution.

Once the investment manager has fully mastered the principles of the New Rule within trust investment, he may find a marketing opportunity offering specialized services to nonprofessional trustees who are less familiar with the area.

For Lawyers

We are in the midst of major trust law and planning reform. The old Prudent Man Rule and the more recent Prudent Person Rule have been replaced by a new conception of a "prudent investor," incorporated in Section 227 of the *Restatement of the Law Third, Trusts* (Prudent Investor Rule), published in 1992. The result is a revision of the ground rules that will govern trust investing for years to come.

In addition, the same modern investment strategies that gave impetus to the New Rule have also generated proposals for reform or expansion of our customary forms of inter vivos and testamentary trusts.[1] Traditional principal and income trust accounting rules are under intense

The comments and example clauses in this chapter are for discussion and are not intended, nor should they be relied upon, as legal advice. The ideas and suggestions are offered for discussion purposes only and should not be used without obtaining independent legal advice on the pertinent federal and state laws and their legal consequences.

[1]Dobris, "New Forms of Private Trusts for the 21st Century," *Real Prop. Prob. & Tr. J.* 31 (1996); Dobris, "Why Trustee Investors Often Prefer Dividends to Capital Gain and Debt Investments to Equity—A Daunting Principal and Income Problem," *Real Prop. Prob. & Tr. J.* 32 (1997); Wolf, "Defeating the Duty to Disappoint Equally—The Total Return Trust," *Real Prop. Prob. & Tr. J.* 32 (1997); Wolf, "Total Return Trusts—Can Your Clients Afford Anything Less?" *Real Prop. Prob. & Tr. J.* 33 (1998).

examination and are very likely to see change, partly due to the New Rule and the growing interest in new types of trusts.[2] Even the traditional law regarding the personal liability of a trustee is being transformed.[3]

These important developments are interrelated and emanate from the redefinition of the fiduciary principles of trust investment management, which is the focal point of the New Rule. This chapter highlights certain issues and observations about the New Rule that may be of interest to lawyers.

The New Rule

For a thorough and helpful discussion of the history, formulation, and goals of the New Rule, we suggest Edward C. Halbach Jr.'s article "Trust Investment Law in the Third Restatement."[4] Halbach served as the Reporter for the Third Restatement and is credited with steering the development of the New Rule through its publication in 1992 by the American Law Institute. His article can be helpful when advising trustees.

Halbach points out that the authors of the New Rule did not intend to endorse any particular theories of economics or investment, and that the main reason for revising the Old Rule was to resolve the conflicts that had developed between its mandates and modern asset management practices. He states that the authors tried to limit the New Rule to the standards needed for trustee and court guidance, while protecting settlor objectives and the interests of trust beneficiaries. This objective, he points out, is achieved in the New Rule by returning to the essence of the generality and flexibility of the Old Rule, while adding modernized principles of trust investment law. In other words, the authors of the New Rule did not intend to completely overhaul trust investment legal principles. The eventual impact of the New Rule may be greater than anticipated by the drafters, depending on how the courts interpret and apply it.

---

[2]Unif. Principal and Income Act (1997 Act), § 104, Trustee's Power to Adjust.
[3]Curtis, "The Transmogrification of the American Trust," *Real Prop. Prob. & Tr. J.* 31 (1996).
[4]Halbach, "Trust Investment Law in the Third Restatement," *Real Prop. Prob. & Tr. J.* 27 (1992).

This explanation of the purpose of the New Rule by its Reporter is important because the Commentary in the Third Restatement also contains several comments that describe certain investment theories and strategies, including Modern Portfolio Theory, passive investing (e.g., "index funds"), and mutual funds. Although the Commentary states that these investment strategies are *not* intended to recommend specific "safe harbor" investment approaches, the fact that they are mentioned might lead some—including a court—to conclude otherwise. Although we share many of the points made in the Commentary about specific investment techniques, we are concerned that, as history has shown, the investment community may eventually develop different views.

Halbach's article also describes the sections of the Third Restatement that are new and those of the Second Restatement that have been revised for clarification and, in some cases, for emphasis. The new sections of the Third Restatement are Section 227, which incorporates the New Rule, Section 228, dealing with how a trustee's investment duties may be affected by the terms of a trust or applicable state law, and Section 229, concerning the duty of a trustee in regard to inception assets of a trust. In addition, twenty-four sections of the Second Restatement were revised because they affected or are affected by the New Rule. Hereafter we will focus only on those aspects of the three new sections and certain of the revised sections that have special significance in the context of reform of the Old Rule.

Basic Fiduciary Principles Imbedded in the New Rule

To emphasize their importance, we reiterate the five basic fiduciary principles that constitute the New Rule. These principles, which we describe in detail in our chapter on the New Rule, are as follows:

1. The duty to *manage risk* in relation to the expected return on an investment or course of action in a trust. This includes the duty to protect a trust's purchasing power against the risks of inflation.

2. The duty to *diversify* trust investments as a way to avoid large losses, unless it is prudent not to do so.

3. The duty to be *impartial* when investing a trust, in respect to the diverse interests of the trust's beneficiaries.

4. The duty with respect to *delegation,* including exercising prudence in selecting delegees, defining the scope of the delegation, and monitoring the delegees' performance.

5. The duty to *manage costs* and to incur only those that are necessary and reasonable.

These five principles, which the Third Restatement describes as a guide for trustees, counsel, and the courts, should be the focus of trustees and their advisors in the coming years. They deal exclusively with the conduct required of a trustee in the areas described. These factors will be the starting point when a court is asked to review a trustee's performance. Hence, every trustee should keep a record of activities. Despite this fairly obvious point, trustees often do not keep adequate records. For the sake of emphasis, we suggest the following "paper trail" procedure and urge lawyers to advise their trustee clients to follow it:

• Record trust investment objectives.

• Record risk/return analyses.

• Record analyses of distribution liquidity needs.

• Record studies of impact of inflation.

• Record considerations of diversification to avoid large losses.

• Record key investment strategies and their rationale.

• Record considerations of impartiality among beneficiaries.

• Record anything important that reflects prudent conduct.

Applicability of the New Rule

A threshold question for lawyers in respect to the New Rule is whether it applies to clients' existing trusts and how it affects the planning and drafting of investment and related clauses for new wills and trusts. This question involves both legal and planning issues. Once the legal issue is resolved (i.e., whether the New Rule applies in the jurisdiction, or can be made to apply if desired), lawyers need to ascertain whether a client wants the New Rule to apply and, if so, whether entirely or only partially. Operating under the Old Rule, with its pervasive restrictions and prohibitive thrust, clients and their lawyers generally agreed that they would avoid those restrictions in wills and trusts, and so lawyers utilized a standard "escape" investment clause. Here is an example of such an investment clause:

> I authorize and empower my Executors with respect to my estate, and my Trustees with respect to any trust hereby created, to exercise from time to time in their sole discretion and without prior authority from any court, in respect of any property forming part of my estate or of any such trust or otherwise in their possession hereunder, all powers conferred by law upon executors and trustees, or expressed in this Will, and I intend that such powers (including the following) be construed in the broadest manner possible:
>
> Without regard to any law prescribing or limiting the investment powers of fiduciaries, power to retain any property of any kind and to invest and reinvest in such securities or other property, real or personal, whether within or without the United States, as they shall determine in their sole discretion, and without regard to diversification.

The same general attitude may not be true when operating under the New Rule. Although the New Rule gives trustees much more latitude and authority than the Old Rule, it has also greatly increased a trustee's responsibilities. In some cases, such as where a settlor will select a family member rather than a professional trustee, the client may choose to alleviate the mandates of the New Rule. This may be wise, pending the interpretation of the New Rule by the courts.

Lawyers may want to change their model clauses to accommodate the probable desires of their clients under the New Rule. Unlike in the past, a single standard investment clause will not likely suffice for drafting purposes. Instead, we may need to have available two types of clauses: one that incorporates the New Rule in its entirety, and another that modifies certain provisions of the New Rule, with the choice as may be appropriate in consultation with the settlor.

Applicability Issues

With the adoption of the Model Act and the New Rule by slightly more than half of the states thus far, lawyers will be faced with the following client situations during this transition period:

1. A settlor or testator wants to use the New Rule for his trusts, but local law has not yet adopted it. Can the New Rule be made to apply to a trust in this jurisdiction?

2. A settlor or testator does not want to use the New Rule for his trusts, or wants to limit its application, and local law has adopted the New Rule as a "default" prudent investor standard (i.e., it applies unless the governing instrument provides otherwise). How should this client's objectives be accomplished?

Attorney Jerald I. Horn of Peoria, Illinois, deals at length with these questions in an article entitled "Prudent Investor Rule—Impact on Drafting and Administration of Trusts."[5] He first cites Section 228 of the Third Restatement, which deals with the relationship of the Prudent Investor Rule to contrary provisions of state law and of a governing instrument. Section 228 provides that when investing trust funds, the trustee (1) has a duty to the beneficiaries to conform to any statutory provisions governing investment by trustees, and (2) has the powers expressly or impliedly granted by the terms of the trust and, subject to certain exceptions, has the duty to the beneficiaries to conform to the terms of a trust directing or restricting investments by the trustee. Against this backdrop, Horn states that the question of whether the Prudent Investor Rule applies to a particular situation

> depends upon (i) underlying state law, (ii) other statutory law that governs investment by trustees, and (iii) the terms of the governing instrument. If none of these prevents the Rule from applying, the Rule applies. Stated differently, the Rule applies by default where State law, federal statutory law, and the governing instrument do not prevent the Rule from applying. This can occur where (i) the Rule is the underlying law of the State and neither any federal statute nor the governing instrument effectively countermands it

[5]ALI/ABA Course of Study, 9/4/97; SC13 ALI-ABA 203

or (ii) the Rule is not the underlying law of the State, no federal statute prevents the Rule from applying, and the governing instrument effectively countermands the contrary law and invokes the Rule.

In the first situation described earlier where the settler wants to use the New Rule but local law has not embraced it, but also does not prohibit it, the trust instrument must provide for it. Horn suggests the following provision:

> Powers of the Trustee. Subject to any limitation of this instrument, without court order, the Trustee may exercise in a fiduciary capacity the powers given the Trustee by this instrument or by law (which, if it does not include the Prudent Investor Rule, shall be deemed to include the Prudent Investor Rule of which the current version at the date of this instrument is set forth in the *Restatement of the Law Third ([Trusts])*).

In the second situation, where the settlor does not wish to use the New Rule entirely but local law has adopted the Rule, and it is a "default" law, the Rule will apply unless the governing instrument contains the settlor's specific or contrary directions that he desires to have apply. If the governing instrument is not explicit, the local Rule will very likely be deemed to apply.

For example, if a settlor wants his trustee to be free to decide whether or not to diversify the trust portfolio in accordance with the New Rule, the instrument should state that there will be no duty to diversify. Or the settlor may decide that the trustee should be free to invest without having to consider whether an investment or strategy is consistent with the Rule's duty of impartiality as to different trust beneficiaries. In that case, the governing instrument should state that the settlor intends that no such duty shall exist with respect to the trustee's investment activities. Although such alterations should be sufficient to convey the settlor's intent that the New Rule is not to apply as expressly modified, some drafters may feel it safer to expressly negate the application of the Rule with additional language such as "The settlor's purpose in granting the foregoing authorities to the trustee is to modify any contrary provisions that may exist in (State's) prudent investor rule or such similar rule of any other jurisdiction that may apply to the trusts hereunder." This is discussed further in this chapter under "The Model Act and Applicability."

If the New Rule has been adopted by a state and it applies to all trusts, and a governing instrument says nothing about the Rule, then presumably it will apply, unless local law requires special language to incorporate it.

Existing Irrevocable Trusts

In existing irrevocable trusts, the question of whether the New Rule applies can raise some difficult interpretation problems, depending on the terms of a trust and the wording of a state's prudence statute. Under the old Prudent Man regime, most governing instruments eschewed otherwise applicable limitations of local law on trust investing. Assume, however, that a state's new prudent investor law is a default statute whose provisions apply only to the extent that a will or trust instrument does not provide otherwise. These situations may raise construction issues in some existing irrevocable trusts. The question will be whether the trust's expressed language takes it outside of the state's prudent investor statute. If, for example, the language in an irrevocable trust clearly and legitimately supersedes a state's old Prudent Man Law, will the trustee be able to delegate his investment duties to an investment agent as permitted by a state's new law? If not, and he does delegate, he may be acting *ultra vires,* possibly resulting in a breach of trust and making him responsible for imprudent actions by the discretionary agent. The answers to these questions are not clear. When in doubt, in the case of existing irrevocable trusts, it may be safer to have a court construe the investment powers of a trust to determine which prudence law applies—the Old or the New. Of course, a state's prudence statute can itself contain construction rules that solve this problem.

The Model Act and Applicability

The Model Act approaches the construction issue by suggesting that *nonexclusive* language will be deemed to invoke the prudence standard of the Act. It provides that certain terms or comparable language used in a trust, unless limited or modified, will be deemed to invoke the New Rule, including such phrases as "legal investments," "authorized investments," "investments permissible by law for investment of trust funds," "Prudent Investor Rule," "Prudent Person Rule," and "Prudent Man Rule." The better drafting approach seems to be for each new trust instrument to expressly describe the settlor's intent—whether to have the New Rule apply entirely, or as the settlor may want it expressly limited or modified. But remember, any contrary provisions of state law governing trust investing that are not or cannot be waived by the governing instrument will be binding on a trust.

The Model Act does not suggest governing instrument language to use when a settlor seeks not to have the New Rule apply. How is one to communicate the settlor's intent in unambiguous language? If a settlor wants to use at least some of the expanded authorities under the New Rule, the authors offer this suggested provision for a will:

> In addition to the powers granted hereunder, and granting investment powers to my Trustee, it is my intention and I so direct that my Trustee, and any of his delegees, shall be held to the prudent investor standard of reasonable care, skill, and caution in the management and investment of the assets of the trusts established by my Will.
>
> Also, I am aware that the State of [   ] has enacted the [State] Prudent Investor Act. Notwithstanding the provisions of that Act, I expressly direct that my Trustee is authorized (but is not directed) in his sole discretion to invest in any type of property, wherever located, including any type of security, improved or unimproved real property, and tangible or intangible personal property, and in any manner whatsoever, whether or not the same shall be authorized or prohibited under the aforesaid Act, it being my intention to relieve my trustee of any mandatory provisions of such Act. I hereby exonerate my Trustee, to the extent permitted by law, from any liability for having failed to comply with any mandatory provisions of said Act in managing the investments of the trusts created hereunder.

The preceding clause should excuse a trustee from having to comply with the mandatory provisions of a state's Prudent Investor Rule, assuming they are waivable, by giving the trustee full discretion on all investment matters, even those the New Rule would otherwise classify as mandatory, while permitting him to exercise discretionary authorities, such as delegation, that the New Rule introduces. The clause attempts to make the terms of the trust, rather than any local law, control prudent investment issues, to the extent that local law permits it. This clause has not been tested for its legal effectiveness, however, and should not be used without making certain that it is proper under state law.

Special Areas of Interest Under the New Rule

"Sole" or "Absolute" Discretion (Section 228)

The Third Restatement, under Section 228 (Comment g), deals with the issue of permissive trust provisions, such as "sole and absolute discretion," and their effect on the scope of a trustee's investment discretion. As discussed earlier, this section provides, generally, that in investing trust funds, while a trustee has a duty to conform to any applicable statutory provisions, he does have the powers expressly or impliedly granted by the terms of the trust, including those directing or restricting investments by the trustee. The comment under that section provides that language such as "sole" or "absolute" discretion will generally broaden a trustee's discretion in investment matters. The authority is not unlimited, however, and a trustee can be held liable if he abuses the extended discretionary authority. In any case, "sole" and "absolute" discretion, or words to that effect, will not permit a trustee to act in bad faith or to disregard the duty of loyalty.

Nonetheless, the phrase "absolute discretion" is exceedingly powerful and for that reason should not be a boilerplate provision. It should be used only when the settlor wishes to give the trustee *the broadest authority possible* beyond the basic prudence requirements of care, skill, and caution, where the settlor's intent and the special purposes of a trust warrant it.

Original Investments (Section 229)

The *power to retain* original investments of a trust is another permissive authority that has to be examined within the context of new Section 229 of the Third Restatement. The typical retention power relates to inception assets and generally authorizes the trustee to hold those specified assets (or categories of investments) for such time and purposes as the trustee sees fit.

New Section 229 of the Third Restatement addresses this area. As for the scope of an *express* power to retain, it gives the trustee more discretion than would exist under the New Rule in the absence of the express power. The settlor's intent governs. On the other hand, the Comment under New Section 229 makes it clear that an express power to retain is not the equivalent of an exculpation provision. The trustee must make a conscious decision to retain any inception assets and must exercise reasonable care, skill, and caution in doing so. A trustee also may be held liable if the power to retain is abused.

Of course, in some situations the settlor or testator wants an asset retained for special reasons, such as in the case of a family business. In such cases, the drafter should not rely on a general administrative power to retain but instead, should use a specific authority to retain. For example:

( ) Power to continue or to permit the continuation of any business, incorporated or unincorporated, which I may own or in which I may have any interest at the time of my death for such period as my Executors or Trustees shall determine, or to recapitalize or liquidate the same upon such terms as in their sole discretion they shall determine, including without limiting the generality of the foregoing power (1) to invest additional sums in any such business event to the extent that my estate or any trust hereby created may be invested largely or entirely in any such business without liability for any loss resulting from lack of diversification, (2) to act as or to select other persons (including any beneficiary hereunder) to act as directors, officers, or other employees of any such business, the same to be compensated without regard to any such person being a fiduciary or beneficiary hereunder, and (3) to make such other arrangements in respect thereof as they shall deem proper.

Power to Delegate, the Requirement of Skill, and the Duty to Control Costs

Delegation The power to delegate is one of the most extensive changes from the Old Rule. The latter allowed very limited delegation by a trustee, primarily for a trustee's administrative or ministerial activities. A settlor could assume that the trustee would personally exercise important duties, such as investing the trust fund and exercising discretionary dispositive powers, such as the power to pay out income or principal and to allocate receipts and disbursements between income and principal.

The New Rule reverses the Old Rule, permitting a trustee to delegate discretionary trust investment *and* management duties. The trustee must be prudent in selecting agents and in defining their scope of authority, however, and must monitor the agents' activities. Clearly, a trustee must personally decide a trust's investment policy and objectives. In other words, he cannot abdicate the entire investment duty.

Skill An interesting related question in connection with the New Rule's delegation authority is whether a trustee who does not possess investment skills *must* delegate those duties to a professional. The Commentary of the Third Restatement makes it clear that the New Rule acknowledges that not all trustees will have the requisite investment skills, and that persons of ordinary intelligence who lack those skills are not prevented from serving as trustees. If, however, a trustee possesses greater skill than persons of ordinary intelligence, he must use it, or be liable for loss from failure to do so. There is no room for lazy professionals.

Although in the case of an unskilled trustee the New Rule does not require the employment of a professional investment advisor, it seems to encourage it. This will be especially important if it becomes common practice among lay trustees. The benchmark measure of a trustee's performance might even become that of other trusts that use professional managers. For lay trustees, using outside professionals can be a form of insurance against liability for bad investment results.

Costs Nevertheless, a trustee's delegation of duties to outside agents must be carried out with a careful look at the cumulative effect of commissions and fees. The New Rule mandates that trustees incur only costs that are necessary and reasonable. If an investment manager is engaged by a trustee, should the trustee adjust his compensation downward? We think so, but there will be exceptions. The Third Restatement does not offer any specific guidelines regarding what will be considered reasonable and necessary costs. To be safe, trustees should keep an eye on average costs being incurred by similar trusts in the trustee's community. A trustee needn't incur the lowest expenses, but he should not be at the top of the heap. If the matter is later examined by a court, comparable costs of similar trusts are sure to be looked at.

Modern powers clauses in wills and trusts usually let a trustee engage attorneys, investment managers, tax accountants, custodians, and other agents to perform services at reasonable costs. These expenses are an important concern to the authors of the *Third Restatement,* as shown by their decision to include the duty to control costs as part of the New Rule itself:

> In addition, the trustee must incur only costs that are reasonable in amount and appropriate to the investment responsibility of the trusteeship.

The Restatement Commentary refers several times to the requirement that a trustee focus on transaction and other investment costs. It emphasizes "long-term investment," presumably to hold down turnover costs, and even the use of index funds to eliminate transaction costs while achieving diversification. Drafters must address this subject with their clients, lest a trustee suppose that the right to engage agents allows him to spend whatever he likes. A trustee who farms out much of the work should probably reflect this in his fee, despite the absence of language to that effect in the trust instrument.

One state, New Jersey, after enacting its New Rule, passed a separate statute specifically directing a fiduciary who delegates investment and management functions to "control the overall costs of the delegation, including making a reduction in the amount of corpus commissions otherwise allowable to the fiduciary which reduction shall take account of the duties and responsibilities retained by the fiduciary with respect to such [trust assets for which investment responsibility has been delegated]" (NJ Stat. § 3B: 20-11.8 [1997]). Other states and the courts are likely to adopt similar formulations.

How should such costs be allocated between income and principal, absent state law on the matter? The trustee's duty of impartiality affects this issue. The answer is to be reasonable. Trustees should make the determination based on the amount of work involved and its value to the income and the remainder beneficiaries, and they should record the rationale behind their determination. Absent that, a trustee who has full discretion in allocating expenses might follow a state's local rule on the matter. For instance, New York allocates trustee fees and related expenses one-third to income and two-thirds to trust principal, unless the trust indicates otherwise. This seems a fair approach.

Executors and Personal Representatives

The Third Restatement declares that it applies to trustees and trusts but says nothing about estates. Does this mean that the Rule does not apply to executors and personal representatives? That is doubtful, although the answer lies with each state's prudence law. Many states do provide that their prudent investor statutes apply to executors and personal representatives as well as trusts, and even other fiduciaries such as guardians and custodians.

Exoneration

With the heightened duties imposed by the New Rule, trustees will have more interest in being relieved of liability. Settlors may especially favor exonerating a spouse and other family trustees from liability.

The Model Act protects a trustee from liability for the acts and omissions of an investment manager to whom he has delegated investment responsibility. This statutory exoneration is conditional on the trustee acting prudently in selecting the manager, in setting the scope and terms of the delegation, and in monitoring his performance. This will doubtlessly encourage lay trustees to delegate their investment duty, and, in the Restatement's view, may even require delegation in certain situations.

As the states adopt the Model Act, one must examine one's state's statute to see if limitations have been placed on the exoneration of a delegating trustee. In Florida, for example, the delegation requires notification to the beneficiaries, which may discourage such delegation. New York has kept a trustee liable for the imprudent acts of a delegee investment manager.

The Restatement makes clear that a trustee cannot be exculpated for breach of the duty to use care, skill, and caution. We have seen trust documents that attempt to give trustees exoneration from liability even if there is willful misconduct, gross negligence, or fraud. We doubt that such a blanket exoneration would protect a trustee from personal liability.

If an attorney is also to serve as a trustee, there may be a conflict of interest if the will or trust he drafts includes an exoneration provision. In those cases, the drafter should make a written disclosure of the potential conflict to the client.

Delegees of trustees may wish to be exonerated from liability for failing to perform prudently. This is also questionable, although the New Rule does not cover it. Since it is doubtful that a trustee can be exonerated for failing to act with care, skill, and caution, it should follow that his delegee may not be exonerated either. In this regard, when a trustee enters an investment account relationship, he should be careful not to unwittingly exonerate or indemnify the investment manager for what is typically described as "all actions other than gross negligence, willful misconduct, or bad faith." This provision is common in investment management agreements, but we question whether a trustee has the authority to agree to undertake such indemnification, and bind the trust assets. Some investment advisors will, if asked, remove such indemnification provisions, as well as another common provision obligating the trustee customer to have all claims against the advisor settled by arbitration rather than judicially. If a trustee cannot eliminate these conditions, perhaps he should consider another investment manager.

Trustee Liability and Measure of Damages

A trustee is liable for making an investment that depreciates in value and results in an actual loss only if there is a breach of duty. Still, on balance, his exposure to liability may have increased under the New Rule because of the higher investment standards it applies.

The Third Restatement made significant changes in the rules governing trustee liability and the measure of damages for losses caused by a breach of trust. Under the Old Rule, a trustee was not allowed to offset or net gains from a breach of trust against losses from multiple breaches of trust. New Section 213 of the Third Restatement continues a slightly modified version of that principle. Liability for a loss caused by a breach of trust still may not be reduced by deducting profit from another and distinct breach of trust. The new section alleviates the situation, however, by providing that if breaches of trust are not distinct and separate, the trustee will be accountable only for the net gain or chargeable only with the net loss. This new principle seems consistent with the New Rule's overall portfolio theory of investing.

New Section 213 is not so accommodating on the issue of the measure of damages. A trustee's liability for an improper investment or course of action will now be measured by reference to the "total return," positive or negative, to reflect the gains and losses in value that reasonably should have been expected from an appropriate investment program. The purpose of the New Rule is to restore the trust fund and its beneficiaries to the position they would have been in had the trust been properly invested.

It seems that this new measure of damages rule comes awfully close to a rule of performance rather than one of conduct, which the New Rule declares itself to be. Of course, the damages rule assumes that the conduct in question was imprudent. In the real world, however, there will be the usual problems of the beneficiaries and the courts relying on hindsight, despite the existence of prudent conduct when the investment was made. This new damages rule will no doubt be a subject for much concern among trustees (and their lawyers). It will certainly put a premium on a trustee's delegating his investment function to an investment manager, preferably one with deep pockets!

Duty of Impartiality

A trustee is duty bound to be impartial as between concurrent beneficiaries within a class and as between successive beneficiaries, unless the terms of the trust provide otherwise. If the duty to be impartial applies to a trust, the trust's investment program will be affected perhaps adversely, by depriving it of capital appreciation that it might enjoy if the trustee did not have to balance the beneficial interests.

The New Rule not only preserves the traditional duty of impartiality but also seems to emphasize it, as if to be certain that it will not be overshadowed by the Rule's liberalizing changes. In planning trusts, lawyers and their clients should specifically address this matter and determine, on a case-by-case basis, whether the duty of impartiality should apply or be modified. In some modern trusts, such as discretionary "spray" or "sprinkle" trusts, revocable trusts, or a trust for a minor that terminates at the age of majority, the duty of impartiality seems out of place. This is especially true if the trustee is given a broad power to invade principal, in some instances even to the extent of terminating a trust. Yet the impartiality rule often binds the trustee and can dramatically affect investment policy in a trust, often causing mediocre or play-it-safe investment strategies so as not to favor one beneficiary over another. But if a settlor wants to play favorites, as in the case of a surviving spouse, the duty of impartiality can thwart the settlor's wishes. These questions should be addressed and handled in the planning and drafting stages of a trust.

The following is a sample clause that attempts to modify the duty of impartiality. The legal effect of the clause has not been tested.

> My Trustees shall, at any time or from time to time, pay or apply so much or all of the net income and principal as my Trustees, in their sole discretion, shall determine to or for the benefit of the Beneficiary, even though any such distribution may terminate the trust and without regard to the interests of any remainderman. In exercising this discretionary power, my Trustees may, but need not, consider the assets and income of the Beneficiary apart from this trust. At the end of each trust year, my Trustees shall add to principal any net income not so paid or applied.

Inflation

The Third Restatement also warns trustees that the effects of inflation must be taken into account when designing a trust's investment program. Its Commentary even suggests that a trustee should seek to make the trust principal grow. That comes quite close to placing a performance gloss on the New Rule's standard of care. There was no similar anti-inflation provision in the Old Rule. Of course, buying growth stocks with high-plowback characteristics and low yields, while a profitable course historically, shifts the company earnings toward capital growth at the expense of dividends. The Third Restatement's extra attention to the future interest of remaindermen tries to push trustees into a more aggressive investment posture than that of past trustees, who were typically conservative and passive, with a bias toward fixed-income investments that favored income beneficiaries while preserving the purely nominal value of principal for remaindermen. This traditional strategy is no longer acceptable.

"Total Return" Trusts

We believe that the duty of impartiality can be served in a better way than the traditional approach, which did something for the income and remainder beneficiaries, but not enough for either. We refer to a "total return" trust, which is described extensively in the articles by Dobris and Wolf cited earlier in this chapter.

The total return approach to investing, which emphasizes lower-taxed capital gains rather than higher-taxed ordinary income, is more tax-efficient than the usual income payment trust. This strategy works best in a discretionary or spray trust with a broad power in the trustee to invade principal for the income beneficiary. The settlor must decide the level of annual payout to the income beneficiary. That payout may exceed the actual income received by the trust, in which case the short-fall is made up through distributions from principal. This is how most substantial individual investment portfolios are managed today. The trustee of a discretionary trust can change the stock/bond investment ratios as circumstances warrant for investment reasons, for the added benefit of all beneficiaries. Hence, a total return trust is entirely compatible with modern investment approaches. For reasons discussed in the following section, however, it is not designed for a marital deduction trust.

Marital Deduction Trusts

A total return strategy should not be used in a marital deduction trust, since it can jeopardize the tax deduction. If, however, the trustee is also given a broad power to invade principal for the spouse for any reason, he can pursue a growth investment strategy so long as there is a reasonable annual income yield. Such a strategy may initially result in a lower ordinary income yield, but it will eventually produce more income than a portfolio devoted primarily to income.

The spouse must receive all of the income to satisfy the marital deduction requirement. If the duty of impartiality is explicitly drafted out, and the trustee has a broad power to invade principal, the spouse can receive a reasonable annual payout consisting of all the annual income plus principal payments to reach the level of payment that the settlor wants. The marital deduction rules are satisfied, the trust has greater growth potential, and income tax is minimized. Everybody wins.

The authors of the Third Restatement express a strong belief in the duty of impartiality, and a trustee must contend with this policy expression. We therefore suggest that, except in trusts where it might serve a particular settlor objective, one should consider drafting a modified duty of impartiality to give the trustee or the investment manager more investment flexibility.

Reformation

Many existing trusts, both revocable and irrevocable, may need a change in their provisions to invoke the New Rule, particularly when state law has not yet adopted the Rule and a settlor of a revocable trust or a trustee of an irrevocable trust wants it adopted. One tends to overlook revocable trusts because of their mutability, but they should be examined while the grantor is living, for two reasons: first, they will become irrevocable upon the grantor's death, and revision then may be unavailable, or at least time-consuming and expensive if court approval is required; second, the grantor might want the present trustee, whether the grantor or an independent person, to have both the duties and the expanded authorities of the New Rule. This will not happen if state law has not adopted the New Rule or if a state has adopted it without making clear whether it applies to all existing trusts. The settlor must take the initiative in such instances.

As stated earlier, application of the New Rule raises special problems for existing irrevocable trusts. If a state has adopted the New Rule and made it retroactive, one must determine whether the terms of a trust correspond to the state's prudent investor law. This can happen if state law demands trust language that adopts the New Rule and the trust document does not contain it or the language is unclear. In these situations, until the matter is clarified by case law, a construction statute, or reformation of the trust, making the New Rule applicable to the trust, the trustee risks acting without authority that is granted by the New Rule. This makes every existing trust a potential construction problem.

Accordingly, some trustees may seek reformation of existing irrevocable trusts if the New Rule's applicability is unclear. This seems appropriate even in jurisdictions where it has been adopted if the intent of the settlor, or interpretation of a trust's language, is unclear.

Generation-Skipping Trusts

Certain existing irrevocable trusts that seek reformation in order to incorporate the New Rule may be grandfathered from application of the generation-skipping transfer tax. That protection might be forfeited if a modification affects the quality, value, or timing of any powers, beneficial interests, rights, or expectancies originally provided under the terms of the trust. A court construction proceeding solely to clarify any ambiguous investment clause of a trust may or may not be deemed a modification fatal to a trust's exemption from the generation-skipping tax. In some situations, even obtaining a private IRS letter ruling before a trust is reformed might be the right move.

Summary

An important question facing lawyers is whether the New Rule requires any changes in approach or language in respect to the thousands of wills and clients' trusts in their files, all of which incorporate each lawyer's favorite investment powers and related clauses. We think it will. Unlike the Old Rule, which eventually was universally rejected as investment policy for trusts by lawyers, their clients, and even the states, the New Rule can generate varying reactions. Overall, the New Rule is a significant improvement in trust investment policy. Its expanded investment authority and flexibility are counterbalanced, however, by some very demanding new responsibilities for trustees, the meaning of which we will not know until the courts interpret the Rule in the years ahead. What degree of diversification will satisfy the Rule? How often is monitoring required, and what is an acceptable level of risk considering the return that is expected and, in a trust context, required? What are unreasonable costs when a trustee delegates investment and administrative activities for the trust? When will a trustee be meeting the Rule's test of avoiding the erosive effect of inflation, or the duty of impartiality in his investment activities?

Some lawyers and their clients may decide to "write their own law" in respect to the scope and duty of investing for their clients' trusts, rather than to invoke the entire New Rule and wait for the courts to decipher its meaning. This pick-and-choose approach may be especially tempting where the trustees are family members, rather than professional trustees, to avoid imposing potential fiduciary liability on the family. Others will embrace the New Rule as entirely salutary. Either way, it is clear the subject should not be relegated to the boilerplate articles of wills and trusts. The policy issues raised by the New Rule are significant, and both lawyers and their clients will be better served by dealing independently with those issues, including whether the Rule itself should be invoked or partially negated, in planning wills and trusts of the future.

For Trustees and Directors of Tax-Exempt Entities

Charitable Trusts and Charitable Corporations

So far we have dealt primarily with private trusts. Trustees of charitable trusts have all of the fundamental duties of trustees of private trusts, as well as the special requirements of the Internal Revenue Code and local state laws that govern tax-exempt or nonprofit entities. Qualified tax-exempt entities are designated as either private foundations or public charities. Most charitable trusts created by individual settlors will be deemed private foundations under the Code. (A public charity—generally, one that receives a certain minimum of its funding from the public—can also be established as a trust rather than a corporation.) So a trustee of private charitable trusts, which will also usually be a private foundation under the federal tax rules, must also comply with those rules.

The distinction between a tax-exempt organization established as a trust rather than as a corporation is more than one of ceremony. The choice between a trust and a corporate form of organization bears directly on the burden of care imposed by the law. In other words, although the purposes of charitable trusts and charitable corporations can be identical, the rules governing the duties of trustees of charitable trusts are significantly different—and more severe—than those of directors of charitable corporations. This anomaly confuses the charitable organization world. The confusion is aggravated by some charitable corporations' way of designating members of their boards as trustees rather than directors. Adding to the uncertainty, the headnotes of the Model Act state that although its provisions do not apply to fiduciaries other than trustees, they are expected to guide the investment responsibilities of directors and officers of charitable corporations.

The Uniform Management of Institutional Funds Act

Trustees and directors of private tax-exempt entities should be familiar with a model statute issued by the Commissioners on Uniform State Laws in 1972, the Uniform Management of Institutional Funds Act (UMIFA). It is reprinted as Appendix 5; a list of states that have adopted it is provided in Appendix 6.

The impetus for UMIFA came from the governing boards of institutions such as colleges and universities that wanted to invest their endowment funds more aggressively than the Old Rule permitted. Unlike private trustees who had the Old Rule to guide them, institutions faced uncertainty about "permissible investments, delegation of investment authority, and the use of the total return concept in investing endowment funds."

Some lawyers advised institutions to follow the principles of private trust law in managing their endowments. Others advised the contrary. Against this background, UMIFA was born. The Act provides the following:

- A standard of prudent use of the capital appreciation in invested funds

- Specific investment authority

- Authority to delegate investment decisions

- A standard of business care and prudence

- A method of releasing investment restrictions through donor acqui-
  escence or court action

The standard of care chosen by the authors of the Act is that of a reasonable and prudent director of a nonprofit corporation, which the authors
correctly deemed more flexible than the Old Rule applicable to private
trusts.

In this book we do not propose to analyze the Act, but rather to call
it to the attention of trustees or directors of tax-exempt institutions. Some
warnings: First, the Act is effective only if it has been enacted by the institution's state. If not, those concerned must look to existing state law. Second, some institutions, such as private foundations, are created in trust
rather than corporate form. UMIFA specifically excludes its own application to charitable remainder trusts, and it may also not apply to an institution that is the sole beneficiary of a trust. In such cases the New Rule
may apply. Remember, the primary distinction is that UMIFA uses the
"business judgment rule" as a standard of care, while the New Prudent
Investor Rule uses the higher trustee standard. However, the authors
believe that the courts will be influenced by the New Rule when examin-
ing the acts governed by UMIFA, since it represents the latest thinking on
these matters.

A whole body of legal principles both in local state not-for-profit
statutes and in judge-made law govern the duties of directors of charitable organizations. The rules are fashioned after similar laws that apply to
directors of business corporations. The business judgment rule, the standard of care that governs a director, has been developed and interpreted
over the years by the courts and incorporated in many state statutes. A
director must exercise the diligence, care, and skill of ordinary prudent
men under similar circumstances, but he is *not* liable for good-faith errors
of judgment in conducting the corporation's affairs. This standard is
much easier to meet than the standard that applies to trustees, who,
although they must also exercise care, skill, and caution, *can* be liable if
loss occurs due to their simple negligence. The exercise of good-faith
judgment by a trustee who acts *negligently* will *not* protect him from liability for loss realized by a trust.[1]

---

[1] Board members obviously prefer to serve under the corporate "business judgment rule" rather
than the higher standard applied to trustees.

By contrast, it has been held that for a director of a corporation to be liable for a breach of the director standard of care there must be *gross* negligence, recklessness, cavalier neglect, and thorough inattention. Thus, it has been primarily owing to the less stringent standard that the charitable corporation, rather than the trust, has become the preferred legal form for charitable organizations. In addition, specific guidelines have developed for business corporations. Unfortunately, some trustees of charitable trusts think that the standard of care for directors of charitable corporations also applies to trustees of charitable trusts. Not so! Charitable trusts (absent contrary federal or state law) require the standard of care and the rules for private trustees, not the less onerous ones for corporate directors. One may wish to convert a charitable trust into a corporation, if state law permits.

Trustees of charitable trusts will be governed by the New Rule, unless local state law has not yet adopted it or the trust's governing instrument provides otherwise. If the New Rule applies to a charitable trust, the trustee will enjoy all of the Rule's authorities, including the power to delegate investment discretion and trust management to outside managers. If delegation is made, the *delegee should be advised* of a charitable trustee's higher standard of care than that required of a director. This is rarely done! Trustees should not assume that investment and other agents will know that difference, and specific written instructions should be used to outline it when the delegee is engaged.

Although separate standards of care govern directors of charitable corporations and charitable trustees, the Model Act may well influence the investment duties of trustees and directors who serve as members of the boards of universities, hospitals, public charities, and the like.

The authors expect this for several reasons. The new Prudent Investor Rule has thus far been adopted by over half the states, and all of them will probably embrace it eventually. The Rule will thus become the universal standard for private trusts. State courts may well look to the New Rule for guiding principles to evaluate the investment activities of charitable corporations. After all, the Rule already applies to trustees of charitable trusts. UMIFA, which governs charitable corporations, and the New Rule, which governs charitable trusts, continue to grow closer together. The law should eventually settle on a single standard. The authors of the Model Act and the Third Restatement hope it will be the

New Rule, of which, therefore, directors of charitable corporations should be well aware.

If there is doubt, board members would seem well advised to use the New Rule as a guide to investing a charitable corporation's funds, rather than to ignore it and hope they are acting prudently. They are also justified in demanding permissible exoneration and indemnification, and insurance to cover it, against personal liability. The stakes are high enough to warrant concern for personal protection.

Some large charitable trusts are often run like charitable corporations, with advisory boards, committees, and other volunteers. Such committee members and others who assist the trustee should be told of their duties as agents. Whether they act with or without compensation, they are governed by the same standard of care that governs the trustees themselves.

Most tax-exempt entities have an investment committee to set policy and supervise delegated managers.

Inappropriate members of such a committee may include persons who have a legitimate interest in the situation but insufficient knowledge of business.

Good members of an investment committee should have a direct knowledge of investment managers, often being members of other investment committees, or be investment professionals themselves and, if possible, have broad business experience.

APPENDIXES

Specimen Trust

This Appendix contains a specimen of an irrevocable inter vivos trust, with marginal notes describing the purpose of each provision of the trust agreement.

It is of the type commonly characterized as a "dynasty trust" because the beneficiaries of the trust include all of the grantor's descendants and the term of the trust will last as long as the rule against perpetuities permits. In this instance, that period is until the death of the last to die of descendants of the grantor's parents, and of the grantor's spouse's parents, who are living on the date of the creation of the trust plus an additional period of up to 21 years. That group of beneficiaries may very well include individuals of three or more generations.

A trust of this type is often created to utilize the grantor's and the spouse's generation-skipping transfer tax exemptions of $1 million each.

By virtue of the extensive term of the trust, the trust property and its future appreciation can be sheltered from estate taxation beyond multiple deaths in a family.

Note: This trust form should not be used except with the advice of legal counsel.

All trusts, inter vivos as well as testamentary, have similar characteristics and form, varying primarily in wordage. Accordingly, this sample should serve as a useful familiarization tool regardless of whether the reader is interested in inter vivos or testamentary trusts, or dynasty or short-term trusts.

Specimen Trust Agreement

THIS AGREEMENT dated the_____day of_____,   **Parties**

and

between_____, as Grantor, and_____as Trustee,   **date of Trust**

WITNESSETH:

WHEREAS, the Grantor desires to create a trust for the benefit of his descen-   **Introductory**

statement

dants and their spouses (hereinafter referred to as the "Beneficiaries"), for the

purposes hereinafter set forth,

NOW, THEREFORE, in consideration of the premises and of the mutual   **Assignment of**

property to Trustee

covenants herein contained the Grantor does hereby transfer, assign, and deliver   **(Schedule A)**

to the Trustee, and the Trustee does hereby acknowledge receipt from the

Grantor of, the property described in Schedule A hereto annexed,

TO HAVE AND TO HOLD the same, together with any additional property   **Creation of Trust** hereinafter received by the Trustee, IN TRUST, NEVERTHELESS, for the following uses and purposes and subject to the terms, conditions, powers, and agreements hereinafter set forth.

Purpose of Trust

FIRST: The Trustee shall hold, manage, invest, and reinvest the same, shall collect the income thereof and shall pay over or apply so much or all of the net

Discretionary power of Trustee over Trust income

income to or for the benefit of a class consisting of the Grantor's descendants living from time to time and the spouses, widows, and widowers living from time to time of such descendants, in such amounts or proportions, equal or unequal, and to the exclusion of any of them, as the Trustee, in his sole and absolute dis-

Accumulate unpaid income

cretion, shall deem advisable. Any net income not so paid over or applied shall be accumulated and added to the principal of the trust at least annually and thereafter shall be held, administered, and disposed of as a part thereof. In addition, the Trustee is authorized and empowered at any time and from time to time

Discretionary power of Trustee to pay principal

to pay over to or apply for the benefit of any then eligible income beneficiary out of the principal of the trust such sum or sums, including the whole thereof, as the Trustee, in his sole and absolute discretion, shall deem advisable.

Authority to hold unproductive property

The Trustee is authorized and empowered to hold as part of the trust any and all articles of tangible personal property and any real property at any time forming a part thereof. The Trustee shall have no duty to make such property productive, and the expenses of the safekeeping thereof, including insurance, shall be a proper charge against the trust.

The trust shall terminate, if not sooner terminated pursuant to the foregoing provisions, upon the death of the last to die of the descendants of the Grantor's parents and of the Grantor's wife's parents living on the date hereof (a list of whom is attached hereto as Exhibit B), and the principal of the trust, as it is then constituted, shall be transferred, conveyed, and paid over to the Grantor's then living descendants per stirpes.

Term of Trust and distribution of Trust remainder

SECOND: If any individual under the age of twenty-one (21) years becomes entitled to a share of the principal of the trust created hereunder upon the termination thereof, the Trustee is authorized and empowered, in his sole and absolute discretion, to transfer, convey, and pay over such individual's share, or any portion thereof, without bond, to such individual or to the parent of such individual or to the guardian of his or her person or property or to a custodian for such individual under any Uniform Transfers to Minors Act or any comparable act pursuant to which a custodian is acting or may be appointed or to the person with whom such individual resides.

Power to hold or distribute shares vesting in minors

Power to distribute to parent or guardian of minors

If the Trustee, in the exercise of his sole and absolute discretion, determines at any time not to continue to hold any property in trust, as hereinabove provided, he shall have full power and authority to transfer, convey, and pay over such property, without bond, to such individual or to the parent of such individual or to the guardian of his or her person or property or to a custodian for such individual under any Uniform Transfers to Minors Act or any comparable act pursuant to which a custodian is acting or may be appointed or to the person with whom such individual resides.

Discharge of Trustee regarding minors' shares

The receipt of the person or corporation to whom any principal or income is transferred, conveyed, and paid over pursuant to any of the above provisions shall be a full discharge to the Trustee from all liability with respect thereto.

Additions to Trust

THIRD: The Grantor, or any other person, may from time to time transfer and deliver, or may bequeath or devise by Last Will and Testament, to the Trustee any property acceptable to him which shall be held and disposed of in all respects subject to the provisions of this Agreement.

Administrative powers of Trustee

FOURTH: In addition to, and not by way of limitation of, the powers vested by law in fiduciaries, the Grantor hereby expressly grants to the Trustee with respect to each of the trusts herein created, including any accumulated income thereof, the powers hereinafter enumerated, all of such powers so conferred or granted to be exercised by him as he may deem advisable, in his sole and absolute discretion:

(1) To retain, purchase, or otherwise acquire, whether originally a part of any trust or subsequently acquired, any variety of real or personal property, any and all stocks, bonds, notes, or other securities, including securities of any corporate fiduciary, or any successor or affiliated corporation, interests in common trust funds and securities of or other interests in investment companies and investment trusts and partnerships (participating therein as a general or limited partner), whether or not such investments be of the character permissible for investments by fiduciaries and without regard to degree of diversification. The Trustee is specifically authorized, but not required, to comply with the provisions of any applicable Provident Investor Act.

Power to invest

(2) To sell, lease, pledge, mortgage, transfer, lend, exchange, convert, or otherwise dispose of, or grant options with respect to, any and all property at any time forming a part of any trust created hereunder, in any manner, at any time or times, for any purpose, for any price, and upon any terms, credits, and conditions; and to enter into leases which extend beyond the period fixed by statute for leases made by fiduciaries and beyond the duration of any trust.

Power to sell, etc.

(3) To borrow money from any lender, including any corporate fiduciary acting hereunder, for any purpose deemed appropriate, including the exercise of stock options, and as security to mortgage or pledge upon any terms and conditions any real or personal property forming a part of any such trust.

Power to borrow

(4) To vote in person or by general or limited proxy with respect to any shares of stock or other security; to oppose or consent, directly or through a committee or other agent, to the reorganization, consolidation, merger, dissolution, or liquidation of any corporation, or to the sale, lease, pledge, or mortgage of any property by or to any such corporation; and to take any steps proper to obtain the benefits of any such transaction.

Power to vote

Power to use nominees

(5) To register any security in the name of a nominee, with or without the addition of words indicating that such security is held in a fiduciary capacity; and to hold any security in bearer form.

Tax elections

(6) To make such elections and exercise such choices under the tax laws as may be deemed advisable, regardless of the effect thereof on any of the interests under any of the trusts created hereunder; no adjustments or transfers between principal and income shall be required as a result of such elections or choices.

Power to settle claims

(7) To pay, compromise, compound, adjust, submit to arbitration, sell, or release any claims or demands of any trust against others or of others against any trust upon any terms and conditions, including the acceptance of deeds to real property in satisfaction of bonds and mortgages; and to make any payments in connection therewith.

Power to distribute in kind

(8) To make distribution of the principal of any trust estate created hereunder in kind and to cause any distribution to be composed of cash, property, or undivided fractional shares in property different in kind from any other shares.

(9) Where granted the power to make distribution of principal from any trust created hereunder, to exercise such power, even if such distribution terminates the trust, and without regard to the interests of any remainderman.

Power to use agents

(10) To employ custodians, investment advisors, accountants, attorneys, and other agents, including any Trustee acting hereunder, and to pay the fees resulting therefrom out of the principal or income of any trust estate; provided, however, that if a corporate fiduciary acting hereunder should retain an individual or another organization to perform services that the corporate fiduciary usually performs as part of its regular fiduciary services, the corporate fiduciary's compensation (as set forth in its published fee schedule) shall be modified so that the total compensation paid for fiduciary services shall be reasonable under the circumstances.

Power to use services of bank or trust company

(11) To place all or any part of the securities which at any time may form a part of any trust created hereunder in the care and custody of any bank or trust company with no obligation while such securities are so deposited to inspect or verify the same and with no responsibility for any loss or misapplication by the bank or trust company; to have all stocks and registered securities placed in the name

of such bank or trust company or in the name of its nominee; to appoint such bank or trust company agent and attorney to collect, receive, receipt for, and disburse any income, and generally to perform the duties and services incident to a so-called custodian account; to employ investment counsel; and to allocate the charges and expenses of such bank or trust company and such investment counsel to income or to principal or partially to income and partially to principal.

(12) To take part in the management of any business in which investment is retained or made and to delegate such duties, with the requisite powers, to any employee, manager, partner, or associate, without liability for such delegation; to reduce, expand, limit, or otherwise fix and change the operation or policy of any such business and to act with respect to any other matter in connection with any such business; to subject to the risks of any such business any part or all of the assets of any trust; to make loans, subordinated or otherwise, of cash or securities to any such business; to select and vote for directors, partners, associates, and officers of any such business; to act as a director or officer of any such business (any corporate Trustee acting through its officers); to deposit securities with voting Trustees; to enter into stockholders' agreements with corporations in which any trust has an interest and/or with the stockholders of such corporations; to sell any such business, any interest in any such business, or any stock or other securities representing the interests of any trust in any such business; to liquidate, either alone or jointly with others, any such business or any interest in any such business; and, generally, to exercise any and all powers as may be deemed necessary with respect to the continuance, management, sale, or liquidation of any such business.

Power to manage a business

(13) To form or cause to be formed, alone or with others, such corporations, partnerships, limited partnerships, and other business organizations organized under the laws of any state or country and to transfer and convey to such business organizations all or any part of the assets, real or personal, of any trust created hereunder in exchange for the stocks, bonds, notes, or other securities or interests of such business organizations.

Power to form corporations, etc.

(14) To abandon any real or personal property which may be determined to be worthless, any such determination by the Trustee to be binding and conclusive on all parties interested hereunder.

Power to abandon worthless property

(15) To execute and deliver any and all instruments to carry out any of the foregoing powers, no party to any such instrument being required to inquire into its

Protection of third parties

validity or to see to the application of any money or other property paid or delivered pursuant to the terms of any such instrument.

Generation-skipping tax provision

(16) If by virtue of any allocation of a Generation Skipping Transfer Tax exemption to a trust created hereunder, such trust would have an exclusion ratio (as defined in Section 2642(a) of the Internal Revenue Code of 1986, as amended, or any successor provision thereto) of less than one but more than zero, the Trustee shall divide such trust into two separate trusts, each representing a fractional share of the original trust corresponding to the trust's inclusion ratio and applicable fraction, respectively, so that thereafter one trust will have an exclusion ratio of one and the other zero.

Exoneration of Trustee

(17) No Trustee acting hereunder shall be liable for any loss or depreciation in value of the trust estate which may result by reason of any authorized action taken hereunder, except as may be a result of such Trustee's negligence or willful misconduct.

Successor Trustees

FIFTH: If the original Trustee named herein should at any time and for any reason cease to act as Trustee hereunder, _____ shall succeed him as Trustee. If he should for any reason fail to qualify or having qualified cease to act as Trustee hereunder, _____ shall succeed him as

Power to appoint a successor Trustee

Trustee. If at any time and for any reason there is no successor Trustee named under this Agreement alive and able and willing to act, the Trustee then acting hereunder shall have the right to appoint an individual or a bank or trust company as successor Trustee by the delivery of a written instrument of appointment to such successor and to the Grantor, if he is then living, or by Last Will and Testament, and any such appointment may be revoked in like manner and a new appointment made.

Each Trustee appointed as hereinabove provided shall have the same estates, powers, discretions, and duties as if originally named a Trustee hereunder.

Any individual Trustee shall have the right to resign as a Trustee hereunder at any time by delivering notice in writing to the Grantor, if he is then living, and to the Successor Trustee.

Right to resign

The expenses of a resigning Trustee's accounting shall be a proper charge against the trust. No Trustee acting hereunder at any time shall be required to give any bond.

Dispensing with bond

Whenever necessary or appropriate in the interpretation of this Agreement, the masculine gender shall be deemed to include the feminine and neuter, and vice versa.

SIXTH: The Trustee may render an accounting upon termination of any trust created hereunder and at such other time or times as the Trustee, in his sole and absolute discretion, may deem advisable. The written approval or assent of all persons not subject to a legal disability then entitled to the net income of such trust and also all persons not subject to a legal disability then presumptively

Accountings by the Trustee

Discharge of Trustee

entitled to the principal thereof, as to all matters and transactions shown in the account, shall be final, binding, and conclusive upon all persons who may then be or thereafter become entitled to all or any part of the income or principal of such trust; provided that if the accounting Trustee is accounting to another fiduciary, then the written approval or assent of such other fiduciary shall be final, binding, and conclusive upon all persons beneficially interested in the estate or

Binding approval by beneficiaries

trust estate represented by such other fiduciary. The written approval or assent as hereinabove specified shall have the same force and effect in discharging the Trustee as a decree of a court of competent jurisdiction; provided that any such written approval or assent shall not enlarge or shift the beneficial interest of any beneficiary of any trust created hereunder.

Relief of duty to account

To the fullest extent permitted by law, the Trustee shall be exempt from any requirement to render periodic or intermediate accountings or inventories.

Irrevocability

SEVENTH: The Grantor has been advised of the difference between revocable and irrevocable trusts, and he hereby declares that this Agreement and the trusts hereby created are irrevocable.

Governing law

EIGHTH: The validity, construction, and effect of the provisions of this Agreement shall be governed by and regulated in all respects according to the laws of

the State of [_____].

NINTH: The Trustee accepts the trusts hereby created upon the terms and con- **Acceptance by Trustee**

ditions herein set forth and consents to act as Trustee hereunder.

TENTH: This Agreement shall extend to and be binding upon the executors, **Binding effect**

administrators, successors, and assigns of the Grantor and upon the successors to

the Trustee.

IN WITNESS WHEREOF, the parties hereto have executed this Agreement as

of the day and year first above written.

_____

, Grantor

_____

, Trustee

STATE OF [_____]

: ss.:

COUNTY OF [_____]

On this _____ day of _____, 19___, before me personally

came_____, to me known and known to me to be one

of the individuals described in and who executed the foregoing instrument, and

he duly acknowledged to me that he executed the same as Grantor.

_____

Notary Public

STATE OF [_____]

: ss.:

COUNTY OF [_____]

On this_____day of_____, 19___, before me per-

sonally came_____, to me known and known to me to

be one of the individuals described in and who executed the foregoing instru-

ment, and she duly acknowledged to me that she executed the same as Trustee.

_____

Notary Public

SCHEDULE A

Specimen Trust Digest

Typically, a trust agreement runs twenty to thirty pages in length. It can be inconvenient for a trustee to turn to the agreement each time a question arises concerning an administrative or dispositive provision of the agreement. A digest of the trust, which is simply a summary of its key provisions, can help a trustee as a ready reference tool, although it should not be relied on as a substitute for the trust agreement.

Specimen Trust Digest

Name of Trust: **Tax ID#:**

_____   _____

Type of Trust:

_____Trust under deed (inter vivos)   _____Trust under will (testamentary)

Effective Date of Trust:

Date of trust agreement:_____

or

Date of probate of will:_____

Probate Court:_____

Date letters trusteeship issued:_____

Name of Creator of Trust:

Grantor, Settlor, Donor, or Trustor (inter vivos trusts):_____

or

Testator (testamentary trusts):_____ _____

NAMES OF TRUSTEE(S):

Sole trustee:_____

Cotrustees:_____

_____

ATTORNEYS FOR TRUST:

_____

_____

Contact:_____

GOVERNING LAW OF TRUST:

State of_____

(Use law of State designated in trust agreement for inter vivos trusts. Use law of

State where will probated for trusts under will. If in doubt, consult attorney.)

REVOCABILITY (INTER VIVOS TRUSTS):

_____Revocable   _____Irrevocable

TERM OF TRUST:

_____Life of income beneficiary(ies)   _____Attained age of beneficiary

_____Date   _____Other

_____

_____

INCOME PROVISIONS:

Beneficiary(ies):_____

_____Mandatory payout   _____Discretionary payout

_____or accumulate: _____Add unpaid income to principal

_____Other. Describe: _____

PRINCIPAL INVASION PROVISIONS:

_____Nonauthorized   _____Authorized

Standard:_____

_____

_____

_____Includes power to terminate trust

POWERS OF WITHDRAWAL:

_____None   _____"5 + 5 Power"

_____Other. Describe: _____

_____

CRUMMEY POWER/NOTICES FOR ADDITIONS TO TRUST:

_____Yes   _____No

_____Conditions: _____

_____

TERMINATION PROVISIONS:

____Powers of appointment. Describe: _____

_____

Final Remainder Disposition:

_____

_____

_____

INVESTMENTS (Describe powers of trustee; special authorizations or limitations):

_____

_____

_____

_____

_____

_____

ADMINISTRATIVE MATTERS (Describe special powers, authorizations, or limitations):

_____Power to allocate receipts and expenses

_____Act by majority vote   _____Power to move situs of trust

_____Other powers/limitations   _____

_____

COMPENSATION:

_____None allowed   _____Special per trust agreement

_____Silent; state law applies   _____Other:

_____

INCOME TAX MATTERS:

State tax situs_____

Trust tax type_____

Ordinary income taxed to_____

Capital gains/losses taxed to_____

Fiscal year_____

MISCELLANEOUS:

_____

_____

_____

_____

The New
Prudent Investor Rule

The New
Prudent Investor Rule

From the *Restatement of the Law Third, Trusts* (Prudent Investor Rule):

§ 227. General Standard of Prudent Investment

The trustee is under a duty to the beneficiaries to invest and manage the funds of the trust as a prudent investor would, in light of the purposes, terms, distributions requirements, and other circumstances of the trust.

(a) This standard requires the exercise of reasonable care, skill, and caution, and is to be applied to investments not in isolation but in the context of the trust portfolio and as a part of an overall investment strategy, which should incorporate risk and return objectives reasonably suitable to the trust.

(b) In making and implementing investment decisions, the trustee has a duty to diversify the investments of the trust unless, under the circumstances, it is prudent not to do so.

(c) In addition, the trustee must:

(1) conform to fundamental fiduciary duties of loyalty (§ 170) and impartiality (§ 183);

(2) act with prudence in deciding whether and how to delegate authority and in the selection and supervision of agents (§ 171); and

(3) incur only costs that are reasonable in amount and appropriate to the investment responsibilities of the trusteeship (§ 188).

(d) The trustee's duties under this Section are subject to the rule of § 228, dealing primarily with contrary investment provisions of a trust or statute.

Uniform Prudent Investor Act

Uniform Prudent Investor Act
1994 Act

§ 1. Prudent Investor Rule.

(a) Except as otherwise provided in subsection (b), a trustee who invests and manages trust assets owes a duty to the beneficiaries of the trust to comply with the prudent investor rule set forth in this [Act].

(b) The prudent investor rule, a default rule, may be expanded, restricted, eliminated, or otherwise altered by the provisions of a trust. A trustee is not liable to a beneficiary to the extent that the trustee acted in reasonable reliance on the provisions of the trust.

§ 2. Standard of Care; Portfolio Strategy; Risk and Return Objectives.

(a) A trustee shall invest and manage trust assets as a prudent investor would, but considering the purposes, terms, distribution requirements, and other circumstances of the trust. In satisfying this standard, the trustee shall exercise reasonable care, skill, and caution.

(b) A trustee's investment and management decisions respecting individual assets must be evaluated not in isolation but in the context of the trust portfolio as a whole and as a part of an overall investment strategy having risk and return objectives reasonably suited to the trust.

(c) Among circumstances that a trustee shall consider in investing and managing trust assets are such of the following as are relevant to the trust or its beneficiaries:

(1) general economic conditions;

(2) the possible effect of inflation or deflation;

(3) the expected tax consequences of investment decisions or strategies;

(4) the role that each investment or course of action plays within the overall trust portfolio, which may include financial assets, interests in closely held enterprises, tangible and intangible personal property, and real property;

(5) the expected total return from income and the appreciation of capital;

(6) other resources of the beneficiaries;

(7) needs for liquidity, regularity of income, and preservation or appreciation of capital; and

(8) an asset's special relationship or special value, if any, to the purposes of the trust or to one or more of the beneficiaries.

(d) A trustee shall make a reasonable effort to verify facts relevant to the investment and management of trust assets.

(e) A trustee may invest in any kind of property or type of investment consistent with the standards of this [Act].

(f) A trustee who has special skills or expertise, or is named trustee in reliance upon the trustee's representation that the trustee has special skills or expertise, has a duty to use those special skills or expertise.

§ 3. Diversification.

A trustee shall diversify the investments of the trust unless the trustee reasonably determines that, because of special circumstances, the purposes of the trust are better served without diversifying.

§ 4. Duties at Inception of Trusteeship.

Within a reasonable time after accepting a trusteeship or receiving trust assets, a trustee shall review the trust assets and make and implement decisions concerning the retention and disposition of assets, in order to bring the trust portfolio into compliance with the purposes, terms, distribution requirements, and other circumstances of the trust, and with the requirements of this [Act].

§ 5. Loyalty.

A trustee shall invest and manage the trust assets solely in the interest of the beneficiaries.

§ 6. Impartiality.

If a trust has two or more beneficiaries, the trustee shall act impartially in investing and managing the trust assets, taking into account any differing interests of the beneficiaries.

§ 7. Investment Costs.

In investing and managing trust assets, a trustee may only incur costs that are appropriate and reasonable in relation to the assets, the purposes of the trust, and the skills of the trustee.

§ 8. Reviewing Compliance.

Compliance with the prudent investor rule is determined in light of the facts and circumstances existing at the time of a trustee's decision or action and not by hindsight.

§ 9. Delegation of Investment and Management Functions.

(a) A trustee may delegate investment and management functions that a prudent trustee of comparable skills could properly delegate under the circumstances. The trustee shall exercise reasonable care, skill, and caution in:

(1) selecting an agent;

(2) establishing the scope and terms of the delegation, consistent with the purposes and terms of the trust; and

(3) periodically reviewing the agent's actions in order to monitor the agent's performance and compliance with the terms of the delegation.

(b) In performing a delegated function, an agent owes a duty to the trust to exercise reasonable care to comply with the terms of the delegation.

(c) A trustee who complies with the requirements of subsection (a) is not liable to the beneficiaries or to the trust for the decisions or actions of the agent to whom the function was delegated.

(d) By accepting the delegation of a trust function from the trustee of a trust that is subject to the law of this State, an agent submits to the jurisdiction of the courts of this State.

§ 10. Language Invoking Standard of [Act].

The following terms or comparable language in the provisions of a trust, unless otherwise limited or modified, authorizes any investment or strategy permitted under this [Act]: "investments permissible by law for investment of trust funds," "legal investments," "authorized investments," "using the judgment and care under the circumstances then prevailing that persons of prudence, discretion, and intelligence exercise in the management of their own affairs, not in regard to speculation but in regard to the permanent disposition of their funds, considering the probable income as well as the probably safety of their capital," "prudent man rule," "prudent trustee rule," "prudent person rule," and "prudent investor rule."

§ 11. Application to Existing Trusts.

This [Act] applies to trusts existing on and created after its effective date. As applied to trusts existing on its effective date, this [Act] governs only decisions or actions occurring after that date.

§ 12. Uniformity of Application and Construction.

This [Act] shall be applied and construed to effectuate its general purpose to make uniform the law with respect to the subject of this [Act] among the States enacting it.

§ 13. Short Title.

This [Act] may be cited as the "[Name of Enacting State] Uniform Prudent Investor Act."

§ 14. Severability.

If any provision of this [Act] or its application to any person or circumstance is held invalid, the invalidity does not affect other provisions or applications of this [Act] which can be given effect without the invalid provision or application, and to this end the provisions of this [Act] are severable.

§ 15. Effective Date.

This [Act] takes effect_____

§ 16. Repeals.

The following acts and parts of acts are repealed:

(1)

(2)

(3)

Uniform Management of Institutional Funds Act

Uniform Management of Institutional Funds Act

An Act to establish guidelines for the management and use of investments held by eleemosynary institutions and funds.

Section
1. Definitions.
2. Appropriation of Appreciation.
3. Rule of Construction.
4. Investment Authority.
5. Delegation of Investment Management.
6. Standard of Conduct.
7. Release of Restrictions on Use or Investment.
8. Severability.
9. Uniformity of Application and Construction.
10. Short Title.
11. Repeal.

Be it enacted . . . .

§ 1. [Definitions]

In this Act:

(1) "institution" means an incorporated or unincorporated organization organized and operated exclusively for educational, religious, charitable, or other eleemosynary purposes, or a governmental organization to the extent that it holds funds exclusively for any of these purposes;

(2) "institutional fund" means a fund held by an institution for its exclusive

use, benefit, or purposes, but does not include (i) a fund held for an institution by a trustee that is not an institution or (ii) a fund in which a beneficiary that is not an institution has an interest, other than possible rights that could arise upon violation or failure of the purposes of the fund;

(3) "endowment fund" means an institutional fund, or any part thereof, not wholly expendable by the institution on a current basis under the terms of the applicable gift instrument;

(4) "governing board" means the body responsible for the management of an institution or of an institutional fund;

(5) "historic dollar value" means the aggregate fair value in dollars of (i) an endowment fund at the time it became an endowment fund, (ii) each subsequent donation to the fund at the time it is made, and (iii) each accumulation made pursuant to a direction in the applicable gift instrument at the time the accumulation is added to the fund. The determination of historic dollar value made in good faith by the institution is conclusive; and

(6) "gift instrument" means a will, deed, grant, conveyance, agreement, memorandum, writing, or other governing document (including the terms of any institutional solicitations from which an institutional fund resulted) under which property is transferred to or held by an institution as an institutional fund.

§ 2. [Appropriation of Appreciation]

The governing board may appropriate for expenditure for the uses and purposes for which an endowment fund is established so much of the net appreciation, realized and unrealized, in the fair value of the assets of an endowment fund over the historic dollar value of the fund as is prudent under the standard established by Section 6. This Section does not limit the authority of the governing board to expend funds as permitted under other law, the terms of the applicable gift instrument, or the charter of the institution.

§ 3. [Rule of Construction]

Section 2 does not apply if the applicable gift instrument indicates the donor's intention that net appreciation shall not be expended. A restriction upon the expenditure of net appreciation may not be implied from a designation of a gift as an endowment, or from a direction or authorization in the applicable gift instrument to use only "income," "interest," "dividends," or "rents, issues or profits," or "to preserve the principal intact," or a direction which contains other words of similar import. This rule of construction applies to gift instruments executed or in effect before or after the effective date of this Act.

§ 4. [Investment Authority]

In addition to an investment otherwise authorized by law or by the applicable gift instrument, and without restriction to investments a fiduciary may make, the governing board, subject to any specific limitations set forth in the applicable gift instrument or in the applicable law other than law relating to investments by a fiduciary, may:

(1) invest and reinvest an institutional fund in any real or personal property deemed advisable by the governing board, whether or not it produces a current return, including mortgages, stocks, bonds, debentures, and other securities of profit or nonprofit corporations, shares in or obligations of associations, partnerships, or individuals, and obligations of any government or subdivision or instrumentality thereof;

(2) retain property contributed by a donor to an institutional fund for as long as the governing board deems advisable;

(3) include all or any part of an institutional fund in any pooled or common fund maintained by the institution; and

(4) invest all or any part of an institutional fund in any other pooled or common fund available for investment, including shares or interests in regulated investment companies, mutual funds, common trust funds, investment partnerships, real estate investment trusts, or similar organizations in which funds are commingled and investment determinations are made by persons other than the governing board.

§ 5. [Delegation of Investment Management]

Except as otherwise provided by the applicable gift instrument or by applicable law relating to governmental institutions or funds, the governing board may (1) delegate to its committees, officers, or employees of the institution or the fund, or agents, including investment counsel, the authority to act in place of the board in investment and reinvestment of institutional funds, (2) contract with independent investment advisors, investment counsel or managers, banks or trust companies, so to act, and (3) authorize the payment of compensation for investment advisory or management services.

§ 6. [Standard of Conduct]

In the administration of the powers to appropriate appreciation, to make and retain investments, and to delegate investment management of institutional funds, members of a governing board shall exercise ordinary business care and prudence under the facts and circumstances prevailing at the time of the action or decision. In so doing they shall consider long and short term needs of the institution in carrying out its educational, religious, charitable, or other eleemosynary purposes, its present and anticipated financial requirements, expected total return on its investments, price level trends, and general economic conditions.

§ 7. [Release of Restrictions on Use or Investment]

(a) With the written consent of the donor, the governing board may release, in whole or in part, a restriction imposed by the applicable gift instrument on the use or investment of an institutional fund.

(b) If written consent of the donor cannot be obtained by reason of his death, disability, unavailability, or impossibility of identification, the governing board may apply in the name of the institution to the [appropriate] court for release of a restriction imposed by the applicable gift instrument on the use or investment of an institutional fund. The [Attorney General] shall be notified of the application and shall be given an opportunity to be heard. If the court finds that the restriction is obsolete, inappropriate, or impracticable, it may by order release the restriction in whole or in part. A release under this subsection may not change an endowment fund to a fund that is not an endowment.

(c) A release under this section may not allow a fund to be used for purposes other than the educational, religious, charitable, or other eleemosynary purposes of the institution affected.

(d) This section does not limit the application of the doctrine of *cy pres*.

§ 8. [Severability]

If any provision of this Act or the application thereof to any person or circumstances is held invalid, the invalidity shall not affect other provisions or applications of the Act which can be given effect without the invalid provision or application, and to this end the provisions of this Act are declared severable.

§ 9. [Uniformity of Application and Construction]

This Act shall be so applied and construed as to effectuate its general purpose to make uniform the law with respect to the subject of this Act among those states which enact it.

§ 10. [Short Title]

This Act may be cited as the "Uniform Management of Institutional Funds Act."

§ 11. [Repeal]

The following acts and parts of acts are repealed:

(1)

(2)

(3)

States That Have Passed the Uniform Prudent Investor Act and the Uniform Management of Institutional Funds Act

A model Uniform Prudent Investor Act ("UPIA") was promulgated by the National Conference of Commissioners on Uniform State Laws in 1994 and recommended for enactment by the states. The UPIA allows trustees and similar fiduciaries to employ modern portfolio theory to guide investment decisions, and evaluates a fiduciary's conduct based on a strategy for the total portfolio, rather than on the selection of individual assets. In addition, the UPIA makes the following alterations in the former criteria for fiduciary investment: (A) the tradeoff between risk and return is identified as the fiduciary's central investment consideration; (B) categoric restrictions on types of investments have been abrogated; (C) the concept that fiduciaries should diversify portfolio investments has been integrated into the definition of prudence; (D) the much criticized rule of trust law forbidding the trustee to delegate investment and management functions has been reversed (some jurisdictions impose notice requirements not mandated by the UPIA); and (E) the trustee may be relieved from liability for acts of the agent, if certain requirements are met.

It should be noted that charitable foundations and private trusts are subject to similar investment rules. The UPIA is applicable to foundations organized in trust form. Charitable corporations, on the other hand, are governed in many jurisdictions by the Uniform Management of Institutional Funds Act ("UMIFA"). The states which have adopted UMFIA are indicated in the far right column of the chart.

State	Uniform Prudent Inv. Act (or most UPIA provisions) Effective Date	Total Portfolio Statutes (minimal UPIA provisions) Effective Date	Authority	(a) Risk/Return Objectives Emphasized	(b) Unrestricted Investment Types Emphasized	(c) Diversification of Investment Types Authorized	(d) Delegation of Portfolio Management as Prudent	(e) Trustee/Agent Investment Management Authorized	(f) Notice of Delegation Severed Trustee/Agent Liability	Uniform Management of Institutional Funds Act (UMIFA)
Alabama		5/16/89	Ala. Code §§ 19-3-120.2 and 19-3-322	No	No	No	Yes	No	No	Yes
Alaska										No
Arizona	7/20/96		Ariz. Rev. Stat. Ann. §§14-7601 to 14-7611	Yes	Yes	Yes	Yes	Yes	No	No
Arkansas	3/31/97		Act 940 of 1997	Yes	Yes	Yes	Yes	Yes	No	Yes
California	1/1/96		Cal. Prob. Code §§ 16045 to 16054	Yes	Yes	Yes	Yes	Yes	No	Yes
Colorado	7/1/95		Colo. Rev. Stat. Ann. §§ 15-1.1-101 to 15-1.1-115	Yes	Yes	Yes	Yes	Yes	No	Yes
Connecticut	6/2/97		Public Act No. 97-140	Yes	Yes	Yes	Yes	Yes	No	Yes
Delaware		7/3/86	Del. Code Ann. tit. 12, § 3302	No	Yes	No	No	No	No	Yes
Dist. of Columbia		2/1/95	D.C. Super. Ct. Prob. R. 5(a)	Yes	Yes	No	No	No	No	Yes
Florida	10/1/93		Fla. Stat. Ann. §§ 518.11 and 518.112	Yes	Yes	Yes	Yes	Yes	Yes	Yes
Georgia		1/1/98	Ga. Code Ann. §§ 53-8-2	No	Yes	No	No	No	No	Yes
Hawaii	4/14/97		30 Hawaii Revised Statutes 554C	Yes	Yes	Yes	Yes	Yes	No	Yes
Idaho	7/1/97		Idaho Code § 68-510	Yes	Yes	Yes	Yes	Yes	No	Yes
Illinois	1/1/92		760 Ill. Comp. Stat. Ann. §§ 5/5 and 5/5.1	Yes	Yes	Yes	Yes	Yes	Yes	Yes
Indiana										Yes
Iowa		4/22/91	Iowa Code Ann. § 633.123	No	No	No	No	No	No	Yes
Kansas	7/1/93		Kan. Stat. Ann. §§ 58-1202 and 17-5004	Yes	Yes	Yes	Yes	Yes	Yes	Yes
Kentucky	7/15/96		Kent. Rev. Stat. § 287.277*	Yes	No	Yes	Yes	No	No	Yes
Louisiana										Yes
Maine	1/1/97		Me. Rev. Stat. Ann. tit. 18-A, § 7-302	Yes	Yes	Yes	Yes	Yes	No	Yes
Maryland	10/1/94		Md. Est. & Trusts Code Ann. § 15-114	Yes	Yes	Yes	Yes	No	No	Yes
Massachusetts										Yes
Michigan										Yes
Minnesota	1/1/97		Minn. Stat. Ann. §§ 501B.151 and 501B.152	Yes	Yes	Yes	Yes	Yes	No	Yes

*applies only to corporate fiduciaries.

State	Date	Citation							
Mississippi									No
Missouri	8/28/96	Mo. Ann. Stat. §§ 456.900 to 456.913	Yes	Yes	Yes	Yes	Yes	No	Yes
Montana	10/1/89	Mont. Code Ann. § 72-34-114	No	Yes	No	No	Yes	No	Yes
Nebraska	4/2/97	Legislative Bill 54	Yes	Yes	Yes	No	Yes	No	Yes
Nevada	4/17/89	Nev. Rev. Stat. § 164.050	No	Yes	No	No	No	No	No
New Hampshire									Yes
New Jersey	3/7/97	N.J. Stat. Ann. § 3B:20-11.1 to 38:20-11.12	Yes	Yes	Yes	Yes	Yes	Yes	Yes
New Mexico	7/1/95	N.M. Stat. Ann. §§ 45-7-601 to 45-7-612	Yes	Yes	Yes	Yes	Yes	No	No
New York	1/1/95	N.Y. Est., Powers and Trusts Law § 11-2.3	Yes	Yes	Yes	Yes	No	No	Yes
North Carolina									Yes
North Dakota	8/1/97	N.D. Cent. Code § 59-02-08.1 to 59-02-08.11	Yes	Yes	Yes	Yes	Yes	No	Yes
Ohio									Yes
Oklahoma	11/1/95	Okla. Stat. tit. 60, §§ 175.60 to 175.72	Yes	Yes	Yes	Yes	Yes	No	Yes
Oregon	9/9/95	Or. Rev. Stat. §§ 128.194 to 128.218	Yes	Yes	Yes	Yes	Yes	No	Yes
Pennsylvania									No
Rhode Island	8/6/96	R.I. Stat. §§ 18-5-1 to 18-15-13	Yes	Yes	Yes	Yes	Yes	No	Yes
South Carolina	6/5/90	S.C. Code Ann. § 62-7-302	No	Yes	No	No	No	No	Yes
South Dakota	7/1/95	S.D. Codified Laws Ann. §§ 55-5-6 to 55-5-16	Yes	Yes	Yes	Yes	Yes	No	No
Tennessee	7/1/89	Tenn. Code Ann. §35-3-117	No	Yes	Yes	No	No	No	Yes
Texas	6/16/91	Tex. Prop. Code Ann. § 113.056	No	Yes	No	No	No	No	Yes
Utah	7/1/95	Utah Code Ann. § 75-7-302	Yes	Yes	No	No	Yes	No	No
Vermont									Yes
Virginia	4/6/92	Va. Code Ann. § 26-45.1	No	Yes	Yes	No	No	No	Yes
Washington	7/23/95	Wash. Rev. Code Ann. § 11.100.010 et seq.	No	Yes	Yes	No	No	No	Yes
West Virginia	7/1/96	W. Va. Code @ 44-6C-1 to 44-6C-15	Yes	Yes	Yes	Yes	Yes	No	Yes
Wisconsin									Yes
Wyoming									Yes

Source: Reprinted with permission from Fiduciary Trust Company International. As of November, 1997.

STATES THAT HAVE ENACTED UNIFORM PRUDENT INVESTOR ACT LAWS
(MARCH 1999)

Alaska	Nebraska
Arizona	New Hampshire
Arkansas	New Jersey
California	New Mexico
Colorado	New York (variation)
Connecticut	North Dakota
District of Columbia	Ohio
Florida (variation)	Oklahoma
Hawaii	Oregon
Idaho	Rhode Island
Illinois (variation)	Utah
Maine	Vermont
Maryland (variation)	Virginia (variation)
Massachusetts	Washington
Minnesota	West Virginia
Missouri	

The chart on pages 180–181 shows the states that have adopted the UPIA, or substantial portions thereof, as of this publication. Additionally, many other states are identified that now require a total portfolio approach to investment management, but which do not otherwise have provisions resembling the UPIA. If a state has no total portfolio statute, the chart makes no representation regarding whether that state's laws contain any other provision resembling the UPIA.

Specimen Request for Proposal

The Model Foundation

TO PROSPECTIVE PROPOSERS:

The Model Foundation invites proposals from qualified firms for portfolio management. Here is our Request for Proposal (RFP) form, setting forth certain requirements. A response must contain the information requested, laid out as specified.

A signed Letter of Intent to Bid on your firm's letterhead in the format of Exhibit _____must reach our office by_____. Facsimile transmissions are acceptable, but not telephone communications. We will answer written questions that you may send.

If you submit a Letter of Intent to Bid on time, you will be mailed the answers to written questions submitted by other potential offerors. If you do not submit a Letter of Intent to Bid on time, you may still submit a Proposal in response to this RFP, but will not receive the answers to the written questions submitted by others.

We look forward to receiving your Proposal.

SECTION I
INTRODUCTION

Background

The Model Foundation is a_____.

As of_____, The Model Foundation portfolio had an aggregate

market value of $_____invested in U.S. equities; $_____in

non-U.S. equities; $_____in long-term fixed-income securities;

$_____in short-term fixed-income securities; $_____in real

estate; and $_____in alternative investments.

Purpose of RFP

The Model Foundation invites qualified firm(s) to provide investment management services in any of the following categories:

A.

B.

C.

While a firm may submit one proposal for any of these categories, each must be submitted separately.

SECTION II
SERVICES DESIRED

The Proposal is for portfolio management services to be provided to The Model Foundation.

A. Investment Objective—To provide returns better than an appropriate benchmark in the categories listed below.

    1.

    2.

    3.

B. Investment Duties—To manage an account subject to investment guidelines including the investment philosophy and process, the investment universe, and indicated portfolio characteristics.

C. Reporting—Monthly, quarterly, and annual written reports to The Model Foundation, which may request individualized report formats and services.

D. Meetings—The investment manager offeror may be asked to appear two or more times per year.

E. Conferences—The consultant should invite The Model Foundation representatives to participate in all group client conferences.

SECTION III
OFFEROR QUALIFICATIONS

III. 1 Requirements

A. The Offeror, with the approval of its legal counsel, accepts the investment advisor contract format.

B. The Offeror agrees to provide the "Services Desired" as detailed in Section II, as well as all other requirements set forth in the RFP.

C. The Offeror must be an SEC-registered investment advisor or an advisor exempt from registration. Form ADV, Parts 1 and 2, or disclosure of the exemption will be provided.

D. The Offeror must have one or more existing U.S. tax-exempt institutional clients invested in the service desired.

E. The key investment professionals assigned to the Account must have a minimum of five years' international investment management experience, and a minimum of three years' experience with the product.

F. The Offeror must be directly responsible for managing the Account.

G. The Offeror must provide assurance that the firm or its key professionals will have no material conflict of interest with The Model Foundation.

SECTION IV
GENERAL INFORMATION

IV. 1 Organization

The Model Foundation is_____.

IV. 2 Definitions

- "Offeror" means an entity intending to submit or submitting a proposal for the Project.

- "Offer" means the undertakings of the Offeror in response to this RFP.

- "Successful Offeror(s)" means the offeror(s) selected by The Model Foundation as the most qualified entity to perform the stated services.

- The "Project" is this RFP and the procedures leading to a contract with the Investment Manager.

- "Investment Manager" means a successful Offeror with whom a contract has been signed and who has begun providing the desired services.

- "RFP" means this Request for Proposal, with any additions, Offerors' written questions and the answers, and any related correspondence that is addressed to all offerors.

IV. 3 Fee

The fee under the contract shall be established by negotiation based on the fees set forth in the Offer. Once the Investment Manager is selected, the fee may be negotiated further. In no event shall it exceed that set forth in the Offeror's proposal.

IV. 4 Time Period

The period of a contract resulting from this RFP tentatively runs from _____to_____.

IV. 5 Eligibility

Neither the Offeror nor a parent company, subsidiary, or affiliate may now be performing consulting services for The Model Foundation, nor may it during the period of this contract.

SECTION V
COMPLETING AND SUBMITTING PROPOSALS

V. 1 Contact

For this Project communications are to be directed, in writing, to:

The Model Foundation

_____

_____

ATTN.:_____, RFP Coordinator
Telephone:_____
Fax:_____

A "Letter of Intent to Bid" on the Offeror's letterhead, and any questions regarding this RFP must be received at the office of The Model Foundation by_____ Eastern Standard Time,_____, 19____. All questions received will be responded to in writing and mailed to all RFP recipients who have timely submitted a "Letter of Intent to Bid." Firms who do not submit a timely Letter of Intent to Bid may submit a proposal in response to this RFP but without receiving the written questions and their answers.

V. 2 Schedule

Event	Date
Mail RFP to Offerors	_____, 19___
Questions due from Offerors	_____, 19___
Letters of Intent to Bid due	_____, 19___
Mail responses to written questions	_____, 19___
Prospective Offerors sending Letters of Intent to Bid	_____, 19___
Proposal due date	_____, 19___
Proposal evaluations and selection of finalists	_____, 19___
Oral interviews of some Prospective Offerors with The Model Foundation staff	_____, 19___

Presentations/interviews of some
Prospective Offerors with
The Model Foundation   _____, 19___

Announcement of successful
Offeror   _____, 19___

V. 3 Submitting Proposals

A. Seven copies are required. Two must have original signatures; five can have photocopied signatures.

All copies shall be sent or delivered to the_____ following on or before,_____Eastern Standard Time,_____, 19___.

Proposals may not be transmitted using electronic media, such as facsimile transmission. Postmarks will not be considered as date received for the purposes of this RFP. Late proposals will not be accepted.

The outside of the proposals' packaging should identify the RFP being responded to.

All proposals and accompanying documentation become the property of The Model Foundation and will not be returned.

V. 4 Format and Content

Proposals should be prepared on 8 ½ x 11 inch paper; however, 11 x 14 inch paper is permissible for charts, spreadsheets, etc.

All of the conditions set forth in this section must be covered thoroughly and completely by the Offeror.

Proposals should be in sufficient detail to permit evaluation and should include tabs separating the following sections:

Section 1: General Information

A. Name, mailing address, and telephone number of legal entity with whom the contract is to be written.

B. Name, mailing address, and telephone number number of primary contact.

C. Name, mailing address, and telephone number of principal officer(s).

D. Legal status of organization (e.g., LLC, sole proprietorship, partnership, corporation).

E. Federal employer identification number.

F. The location of the office from which the Offeror will operate.

G. Qualifications Compliance Certificate (Exhibit "G" attached hereto).

Section 2: Descriptive Essay

Include a brief essay as outlined below, separate from the Questionnaire. It will be used during the oral interviews. It should not be in the form of references to sections of the Offeror's overall Proposal.

A. Organization:
    Brief history of your firm, including year organized, when it began managing U.S. tax-exempt assets, its ownership, and information on affiliated companies or joint ventures. Describe the key professionals' investment experience related to the Account. Describe the compensation structure, especially as it applies to professionals who do not have equity participation. Discuss turnover of key investment professionals over the past five years.

B. Philosophy:
    Describe the investment philosophy of the firm and explain how value is added over a passively managed portfolio. Describe the process of constructing and maintaining a portfolio, including security selection, risk controls, and sell disciplines. Define the universe of stocks from which the firm selects. What gives the firm a competitive advantage?

C. Resources:
    Describe the firm's resources, particularly the research staff, portfolio managers, client service representatives, and administrative staff. What percentage of research is generated internally and what percentage externally? Describe information management systems, including research databases, tracking systems, and portfolio accounting and client reporting systems.

Section 3: Questionnaire

Complete and include the Questionnaire attached.

Section 4: Warranties

The Warranties form attached must be signed by the president or chief executive officer of a corporation or LLC, the managing partner of a partnership, the proprietor of a sole proprietorship, or all members of a joint venture, and included in the Offeror's Proposal.

Section 5: Supplemental Information

An Offeror may provide supplemental information and/or documentation.

Section 6: Fee Proposal

The Model Foundation intends to enter into a three-year contract with the selected Offeror(s). The fee must constitute part of the Proposal. The services detailed in Section II-2 of this RFP are the basis for the proposed fee. In no case will the negotiated fee be higher than the fee contained in the proposal.

V. 5 Proprietary Information

Proposals will remain confidential until any successful Offeror(s) resulting from this RFP is announced. Thereafter, proposals will be deemed public record. In the event that an offeror desires to claim portions of its proposal as exempt from disclosure it should clearly identify those portions in a proposal transmittal letter. The transmittal letter must identify the page and particular exemption(s) from disclosure upon which it is making its claim. The word "CONFIDENTIAL" must be printed on the lower right-hand corner of each page claimed to be confidential. The entire proposal may not be designated as confidential.

V. 6 Records Retention

After the date of the announcement of the successful Offeror(s), The Model Foundation will retain for five years one master copy of each Proposal received.

V. 7 Preparation and Travel Costs

The Model Foundation will not be liable for an Offeror's costs in preparing and presenting a proposal submitted in response to this RFPP.

The Offeror assumes responsibility for travel and associated costs relating to bidding on this Project.

V. 8 Proposal Evaluation Procedure

The Model Foundation reserves the right to reject all proposals without penalty.

A.   The Model Foundation will review each proposal for compliance with the

Offeror's Requirements stipulated in this RFP. Noncompliant Proposals will not be considered.

B. The evaluation team will identify Offerors to be considered for interviews.

V. 9 Addenda to the RFP

If this RFP needs to be revised, such revisions will be provided to all Offerors who have submitted timely Letters of Intent to Bid; after submission, no amendments will be possible. Proposals should not consist solely of marketing materials.

SECTION VI
RIGHTS

VI. 1 Proposal Review Criteria

All determinations of clarity and completeness in the responses will be made solely by The Model Foundation, which may seek clarification or additional information.

VI. 2 Contract Award

Should The Model Foundation fail to negotiate a contract with its first choice among the Offeror(s), it may negotiate and contract with another Offeror, or with more than one Offeror.

VI. 3 Publicity

There must be no publicity before a contract is signed.

VI. 4 Equal Opportunity

Offerors required by state or federal law to have affirmative action plans may be asked to provide copies of their current affirmative action plan, and any evaluation of that plan.

SECTION VII
MISCELLANEOUS TERMS AND CONDITIONS

VII. 1 Successful Offeror Notification

On or about the date specified in Section V.2, "Schedule of Procurement Activities," of this RFP, a letter indicating whether the Offeror was selected as "the apparently successful offeror" will be mailed to each Offeror.

WARRANTIES

The Offeror warrants the following:

1. **Independent Cost Determination**
   Prices and cost data have been arrived at independently, without consultation with any other Offeror or competitor in order to restrict competition, although an Offeror may join with other persons or organizations to present a single proposal.

2. **"Most Favored Nation" Warranty**
   Charges to The Model Foundation do not exceed those charged any other client for the same services.

3. **Conflicts of Interest**
   The Offeror warrants that no conflict of interest exists with respect to the Offeror, or any of its employees, regarding any current or past relationship with The Model Foundation.

4. **Offer Validity Time**
   Any Proposal is a firm offer for 120 days and may be accepted without further negotiation within that time.

5. **References**
   The Model Foundation is granted permission to contact any references provided in response to this RFP.

6. **Acceptance**
   The Offeror, by submission of a response to this RFP, accepts the Terms and Conditions in this RFP as part of the final contract, if selected.

The person(s) signing below warrant the truth of all of the foregoing warranties and responses.

_____   _____
Signature   Firm

_____   _____
Title   Date

Specimen Preliminary Management Questionnaire

SPECIMEN PRELIMINARY MANAGEMENT QUESTIONNAIRE

1. Firm name

    Address

    Telephone

    Fax

    E-mail

    Contact person

    Direct line

    Principal owners of firm, with percentage shares

    Enclose brief financial statement of firm

2. Assets under management

    Stocks

    Bonds

    Other

    Total

3. (a) Service or product contemplated, with brief characterization of investment philosophy

    (b) Earliest date when this service or product was offered by this firm

    (c) Quarterly total returns since inception for this service or product

(d) Most appropriate benchmark

(e) Historical excess return versus the benchmark

(f) Number of accounts to which service or product is currently provided

(g) Aggregate assets of these accounts

(h) Is the service or product available via an existing commingled vehicle?

( ) Yes   ( ) No

If yes:

(a) Name

(b) Description (mutual fund, partnership)

(c) Onshore or offshore?

(d) Frequency of entry   ( ) Daily   ( ) Weekly

( ) Monthly ( ) Quarterly

(e) Frequency of exit   ( ) Daily   ( ) Weekly

( ) Monthly ( ) Quarterly

(f) Minimum initial investment

4. Other considerations

(a) Fee schedule

(b) Incentive fees accepted?

(c) Short sales used?

(d) Derivatives used?

5. List persons who exercise continuous judgment:

Percentage of Working Hours Devoted to:

Name	Years in Position	Investment Tasks*	Noninvestment Tasks**	Outside Directorships, Pro Bono, etc. (List)

*portfolio management, investment research and trading.

**administration, marketing, etc.

6. Average dollar amount and number of accounts per manager

7. Please enclose one example of a response to a full-scale questionnaire from another client.

Specimen Extensive Management Questionnaire

SPECIMEN EXTENSIVE MANAGEMENT QUESTIONNAIRE

A. ORGANIZATION

1. Name

    Address

    Telephone

    Fax

    Contact person

2. Nature of firm (check)

    Bank/trust co.____   Broker affiliate____

    Bank affiliate____   Joint venture____

    Merchant bank affiliate____   Independent investment couselor____

    Investment bank affiliate____   Insurance company____

    Broker____   Other (*specify*)____

3. History of firm; date of SEC registration.

4. Ownership structure (check one):

    Publicly owned____   Partnership____   Employee-owned____

    Subsidiary of_____   Other_____

5. Describe changes in the ownership structure in the last ten years.

6. Enclose latest year-end financial statements.

7. If any entities or individuals apart from the professionals currently active in the firm have a significant ownership stake (greater than 10 percent) in the company, list:

Name of Entity/Group	% Ownership
_____	_____
_____	_____
_____	_____
_____	_____

8. With which regulatory agencies is the company registered?

 ____SEC   ____NASD   ____DFTC   ____None

9. Location, opening date, and function(s) of other offices.

10. Amount and nature of client funds managed.

B. CONTROLS

1. Levels of insurance coverage for fidelity bonds, errors and omissions coverage, and other such coverage with insurance carriers.

2. Has the firm or the responsible individuals ever been out of compliance with the SEC, NASD, or any other regulatory agencies? Yes____ No____ If yes, describe.

3. Has the firm or any office or principal been involved in investment-related litigation or unfavorable publicity? Yes____ No____ If yes, describe.

4. Is the firm's investment research sold to outside clients? Yes____ No____ If yes, describe arrangement.

5. When was the company last reviewed by a regulator?_____

6. What were the significant findings and recommendations?

7. When is the next review expected to take place?_____

8. Does the firm have a dedicated compliance function in-house?

Part-time_____   Full-time_____   No_____

Name of compliance officer_____

9. Does the company have a dedicated internal audit function?

Yes_____ No_____

Name of department head_____

10. Is the company audited by an independent audit firm?

Yes_____ No_____

Name of audit firm_____

11. Does the company receive a management letter from its auditors?

Yes_____ No_____

12. Is an Internal Control Report issued for the company?

13. Are persons with trading authority required to take vacations annually?

Yes ____ No ____

14. Do any persons with trading authority also maintain client account records?

Yes_____ No_____

15. How are the company's account records reconciled to records maintained by the custodian for this account?

	Daily	**Weekly**	**Monthly**	**Quarterly**
Cash				
Securities costs and market values				

16. Does the company independently monitor dividends and stock splits for equities held in the account?

Yes_____ No_____ Rely upon custodian for notification_____

17. Does the company have a written recovery plan in the event of fire or communications or information systems failure?

Yes_____ No_____

C. Personnel

1. Number of professionals managing assets for U.S. clients:

	Total	Office Location
Portfolio managers		
Equity		
Fixed income		
Research analysts		
Equity		
Bond markets		
Trading		
Marketing/client servicing		
Other		
Economists		
Administration		
General executives		
Total Professionals		

2. List professionals who might manage this account:

Percentage of Time

Name	Years since became key decision maker	Noninvestment-related tasks	Outside investment-related tasks	This account	Outside directorships, pro bono, etc.

D. Assets Under Management

1. Investment management services offered to U.S. clients:

	Tax-Exempt Separate Accounts		Taxable Separate Accounts	
	Number	Value	Number	Value
All fixed income				
U.S. large cap growth				
U.S. small cap growth				
U.S. large cap value				
U.S. small cap value				
European (including UK) Large cap				
European (including UK) Small cap				
EAFE				
Total EAFE				
Latin America				
Emerging markets not listed above				

Total U.S. Client Accounts:

5. Corporate equity investment performance by quarter for ten years. Time-weighted, nonannualized, net of fees, expenses, and transaction costs:

   Exclude returns from cash and equivalent reserves. Weight calculations for account size. Include all discretionary accounts, including those no longer with the firm. Make no alterations of composites.

   Do these returns comply with AIMR Performance Presentation Standards?

   Describe any independent performance audits.

6. Portfolio characteristics of corporate equity portfolio, or appropriate fund, as applicable:

    a.   Market capitalization ($millions) % of Portfolio

        Over $50,000

        $10,000 to $50,000

        $2,000 to $10,000

        $1,000 to $2,000

        $500 to $1,000

        Less than $500

    b.   Average P/E ratio

    c.   Five-year EPS growth rate

    d.   Five-year dividend growth rate

7. Provide a recent representative portfolio.

8. List ten largest holdings firm-wide.

9. Enclose latest ADV form.

10. Does the firm use outside new business consultants?

11. Please provide three appropriate client references: name, address, telephone, fax, individual to contact.

E. FIRM STRATEGY AND TACTICS

1. Brief description, including significant areas of geographic or industry concentration; growth or value preference; other criteria.

2. Diversification; percentage limits per company, industry, etc.

3. Buying disciplines.

4. Selling disciplines.

5. Are decisions top-down, bottom-up, fundamental, quantitative, or other? Is technical analysis or MPT employed?

   Describe.

6. Strategic partners and co-investors.

7. Targeted holding period(s).

8. Risk controls: country, currency, concentration, etc.

9. Has value added against index been achieved by stock, country, currency, or market selections?

10. How is cash held?

11. Provide personal trading/conflict-of-interest policy.

12. Does the firm lend securities?

Pricing System

Investment	Pricing Source(s)	Frequency	Entity Responsible
Domestic equities			
Domestic fixed income (government agency, corporation, municipal)			
International equities (developed)			
International equities (emerging)			
International fixed income (developed)			
International fixed income (emerging)			
CMOs			

Pricing System

Investment	Pricing Source(s)	Frequency	Entity Responsible
Futures			
Options (listed or private)			
Interest rate swaps/ equity swaps			
Limited partnership interests			
Other			

F. Costs

1. Annual fees: Paid when?

2. "Most favored nation" features, if any

3. Preferred custody arrangements and costs

4. Brokerage arrangements and costs

5. Annual account turnover for last three years

6. Does the firm or its parent have a direct or indirect interest in securities brokerage? Yes____ No____ If so, describe.

7. Policy on soft dollars.

8. What is brokerage allocation policy?

9. Can clients direct brokerage?

G. Investor Base

1. Names or categories of past and current clients; approximate size of commitment(s); vehicle(s) utilized.

2. Renewal rates.

3. Current fund-raising efforts.

H. CLIENT SERVICE AND REPORTING

1. Frequency and nature of investor reports and meetings.

2. Nonroutine reports and services.

3. Back-office staffing and controls.

4. Outside professional service providers: attorneys, auditor(s), others.

Specimen Investment Management Agreement

Although many private trustees have engaged professional investment managers over the years, we expect the practice to increase under the new Prudent Investor Rule, which, unlike the Old Rule, authorizes private trustees to delegate their investment duties to investment managers. This will usually involve a formal agreement. They differ greatly. In the chapter on administrative matters, we stressed the importance of scrutinizing a manager's account agreement form, particularly in such areas as the standard of care that will govern the manager (it should correspond to the trustee's), the procedure for settling claims (one should avoid a commitment to use arbitration), indemnification clauses (which should be avoided wherever possible), and reporting and monitoring procedures. This Appendix[1] contains a sample investment management agreement designed for a "nondiscretionary" fiduciary investment account where the trustee must approve all investment recommendations. A "discretionary" account form would be the same, except it would provide that the manager could make investment changes without the trustee's prior approval.

---

[1]Adapted from a Brown Brothers, Harriman form.

Specimen Investment Management Agreement

To: Investment Manager   Date:

Dear Sirs:

Please establish an Investment Advisory Account ("Account") in the name of the undersigned, upon the following terms and conditions:

1.   Investment Account.

As provided in this agreement, Investment Manager (hereinafter "IM" or "you") shall be responsible for providing continuing review and analysis of general business, security market, monetary, industrial, and other relevant investment considerations for the benefit of the assets in the account ("Account Assets"). You may also from time to time exclude from the service such of the securities included in the Account Assets that you cannot adequately analyze. Such securities may be carried as "Assets not under Review" or "Private Assets" and shall not be subject to an investment advisory fee.

You will provide investment recommendations for the Account Assets, in a manner you believe generally consistent with the investment objectives and restrictions that are provided to you in writing.

You will execute purchase, sale, or other investment changes only after the undersigned has directed you to do so.

2.   Custodianship and Safekeeping.

Custody and safekeeping will be provided by_____ and covered by a separate agreement.

3. Account Reports.

You will provide periodic investment reports that will include (1) a listing of the Account Assets held in the Account at the end of the reporting period, with costs and market values, (2) a listing of transactions in the Account during the period, and (3) a schedule of income generated in the Account during the period. You may also provide any additional reports that are mutually agreed upon, such as tax information.

4. Compensation.

For your services under this agreement, you will receive the compensation set forth in Schedule A, appended to this agreement.

You will also notify the undersigned at least thirty days in advance of any change in your schedule of fees and charges applicable to the Account.

5. Potential Conflicts.

In effecting security transactions for the portfolio you will seek to obtain the best price and execution of orders. Nevertheless, the undersigned acknowledges that you render advice to and execute transactions for the account of persons other than the undersigned, at other prices and amounts, or relating to securities that are not purchased or sold for the Account. You may combine trades for the Account with trades for your other accounts. In the event that trades are combined, each trade will be averaged as to price and equitably allocated among accounts involved in the trade. All transactions will be conducted in accordance with law and applicable rules and regulations.

6. Termination of Agreement.

This agreement may be terminated by you or the undersigned at any time, upon receipt of thirty days' prior notice in writing. Your compensation will be prorated through the date of actual termination of the Account.

7. Disclosure Documentation.

The undersigned acknowledges receipt of your Investment Advisory Client Disclosure Document.

8. Governing Law, Amendment, No Assignment.

This agreement is governed by the laws of the State of New York and is binding upon the undersigned's successors, estate, heirs, assigns, and personal representatives. It may be amended or modified only in writing. This agreement may not be assigned by you or the undersigned without mutual written consent.

9. Notices, Communications, Mailings.

All reports, notices, and other written communications will be sent to the address indicated below, unless you are otherwise notified in writing.

> If to IM: [Investment Manager]
>
> Attention:

> If to the undersigned:
>
> Attention:

You will notify the undersigned, in writing and within a reasonable period of time, of all changes in the membership of the IM partnership [or major shareholder changes if IM is a corporation].

10. Fiduciary Account.

If the Account is established by the undersigned in a fiduciary capacity, the undersigned represents and certifies that (a) all beneficial interests in the estate, trust, or other relationship for which the undersigned is acting as such fiduciary are owned by individuals or by nonprofit organizations, or otherwise as you are notified by the undersigned, and (b) the undersigned is legally empowered to enter into this agreement in such capacity, to obtain your services, and to grant you authority and undertake the obligation provided hereunder.

The undersigned represents that any and all necessary approvals for the Account are either indicated by the signature to this agreement or have been obtained by the undersigned.

The undersigned agrees to provide you with a true copy of the instrument governing the fiduciary capacity of the undersigned, and to notify you within thirty days thereof, of any changes or amendments to such governing instrument which affects this account relationship in any manner.

11. Account Authorization.

If the Account is established by a corporation or a partnership, the undersigned represents that this agreement has been duly authorized by a resolution of its Board of Directors or by written approval of the partnership, as the case may be, which resolution of the Board of Directors or written approval of the partnership also authorizes the undersigned to sign on behalf of such corporation or such partnership. A true and complete copy of the applicable resolution, or written partnership approval, is attached.

12. Severability.

No term or provision of this agreement that is invalid or unenforceable in any jurisdiction will render invalid or unenforceable in that jurisdiction the remaining terms or provisions of this agreement, or its terms or provisions in any other jurisdiction.

Yours sincerely,

1._____

    Printed name of account owner
    [See examples below.*]

[Use this column if two
signatures are required.]

2._____   _____

    Signature   Signature

3._____   _____

    Printed name   Printed name

* **Examples**
  * John Doe, individually
  * John Doe & Mary Doe, joint tenants with right of survivorship
  * J. Doe & M. Doe, as tenants in common
  * M. Doe, custodian for J. Doe, Jr., a minor
  * XYZ Corporation
  * ABC and Co.
  * DEF Manufacturing, LLC.
  * John Doe & GHI Trust Co., trustees for J. Doe, Jr. U/A 1/2/99
  * John Doe, executor under the Will of Emily Doe

4._____ _____
   Capacity   Capacity

Please enter the capacity in which you are signing if other than individually or as joint tenant (examples: corporate officer, general partner, trustee, executor, guardian, attorney-in-fact).

5._____ _____
   Date   Date

Accepted and agreed:

_____
For Investment Manager

_____
Printed name and title

_____
Dated

Account no._____

Specimen Statement of Investment Objectives

The new Prudent Investor Rule requires private trustees to establish an overall investment strategy. The best way to demonstrate that a trustee has addressed this obligation is through a written statement of investment policies. This Appendix offers a sample of a statement that is geared to a private trust with outside professional investment management.

SPECIMEN
TRUST UNDER WILL OF _____
FOR THE BENEFIT OF _____.

Overview:

- The following statement of general investment objectives and policies constitutes guidelines for the overall management of the Trust's assets by investment managers as the Trustees shall select from time to time.

- The central objective is to preserve the real (inflation-adjusted) purchasing power of the Trust's assets while providing for long-term growth of principal and income without undue risk.

Asset Allocation Guidelines:

Equities: 70% (of which up to 20% of the 70% may be non-U.S. equities, but not more than 5% of the 70% shall be emerging markets equities)

Fixed income: 35%

The overall portfolio assigned to each investment manager will be targeted to the ratios reflected above, but each manager has discretion to have up to 75% of the portfolio allocated to equities. Additionally, within asset sectors, the allocations may vary +/- 5 percentage points on a short-term basis.

Income Requirements:

The overall portfolio assigned to each manager willl be invested so as to achieve a minimum targeted yield of [x]% based on the market value of the portfolio.

Equity Guidelines:

- A majority of the Trustees must pre-approve investments in private placements, venture capital, futures, options, or any derivative invest-ments by a manager.

- Short sales are prohibited.

- No more than 5% of a corporation's outstanding issues in a given security class may be purchased.

- No single issue may comprise more than 10% of the portfolio assigned to an investment manager.

Fixed-Income Guidelines:

- Non-U.S. Government (or U.S. Government Agency) issues must be invest-ment grade (rated at least Baa by S&P or BBB by Moody's) at the time of purchase.

- A single security (excluding U.S. Government and Government Agency issues) may not comprise more than 10% of the portfolio at cost.

- Cash and equivalents should be in money market funds or securities rated at least A-1 by S&P or P-1 by Moody's.

- The weighted average maturity of fixed-income securities shall not exceed five years, with the final maturity of any security limited to seven years.

Performance Benchmarks:

Domestic equity:	S&P 500
International equity:	EAFE
Fixed income:	Lehman Brothers Government/Corporate Index
Cash:	Three-month T-bill

Investment activity and results will be monitored by the Trustees on a continu-ing basis, but investment performance will be evaluated on a long-term basis over at least a market cycle, which is generally three to five years. Each manager will be expected to provide (1) monthly reports of investment transactions and positions, and (2) performance reports, on an after fees basis, no less than every six months.

Meetings:

Each investment manager is expected to meet with the Trustees at least two times per year.

Acknowledged by:

By: _____   Date: _____
    Investment manager

Checklist for Monitoring an Investment Account

CHECKLIST FOR MONITORING AN INVESTMENT ACCOUNT

1. **Structure.** A prudent monitoring system should do the following:

    *   Provide needed information and date about the investment manager's activities

    *   Include an analysis of that information

    *   Integrate the data and the analysis into meaningful findings and conclusions, which the trustee uses to evaluate the delegee's actions and to measure the manager's performance toward achieving the objectives of the trust

2. **Periodic meetings.** The Trustee should arrange a schedule of periodic meetings with the investment advisor. How often depends on the size and complexity of the trust portfolio. New relationships require more contact in the early stages.

    Get monthly or quarterly statements of the account's investment activity and holdings. At minimum, hold semiannual meetings with the advisor, and more frequent meetings during volatile market conditions. Prepare memoranda of meetings and retain them in the trust's records.

3. **Risk measurement.** Establish risk parameters for the trust; incorporate them in the trust's written statement of investment policies and objectives; communicate them to the investment advisor. Measure risk performance against parameters when monitoring overall activity of the advisor.

4. **Investment performance.** Measure the advisor's performance against appropriate market indices; compare it with the advisor's peers; most important,

evaluate it against the specific objectives of the trust. Measure the advisor's market performance at one-, three-, and five-year intervals, and more frequently if performance is mediocre. Change the advisor if performance is consistently below that of his peers.

5. **Asset allocation.** Set parameters in the trust's written investment policy statement. Look for major shifts from parameters; ask the advisor to explain and justify them.

6. **Quality ratings.** Set minimum quality investment ratings in the trust's written investment policy statement. Look for deviations from policies; demand exception reports from the advisor when the ratings parameters are breached.

7. **Portfolio turnover rate and transaction costs.** If the annual portfolio turnover rate is greater than 75 to 100 percent, determine the reasons and measure cost-benefit.

8. **Tax efficiency.** Determine the short-term versus long-term capital gains tax experience; measure tax efficiency for the overall portfolio as part of the investment performance results.

9. **Maturities/duration/credit quality.** Look for any unusual patterns or variations from the trust's investment policy statement concerning maturity/duration schedules and the credit ratings of fixed-income security holdings.

10. **Industry sectors.** Look for any significant changes from policy or from the advisor's usual philosophy.

11. **Above-average market performance.** Determine if this results from the manager taking greater risks than is suitable for the trust.

12. **Portfolio concentration.** Determine if the trust's portfolio is adequately diversified in accordance with the general thrust of the Prudent Investor Rule.

13. **Price-earnings ratios.** Determine if the advisor's holdings reflect price-earnings ratios that are inappropriate for the trust's risk tolerance.

14. **Holding periods.** Measure average holding periods of portfolio securities to determine if the manager's sell discipline is too conservative.

15. **Liquidity risk.** Determine the marketability of the trust's portfolio vis-à-vis the needs of the trust.

16. **Leverage.** Determine if leverage *is* being used, if it *should* be used, and, if so, if the advisor is acting prudently in leveraging the portfolio.

17. **Derivatives, other alternative media.** If the trust's policy statement allows derivatives, and the manager is using them, determine that the advisor has the ability to manage them, and complies with the limits set for the trust.

18. **Risk performance.** Develop a system to measure the manager's investment performance results against the degree of risk being taken, to determine if the latter is justified.

Form ADV, Uniform Application for Investment Adviser Registration

This very detailed form is available from every registered investment adviser, and it contains information important for a client. Thus, we hold any trustee to be failing in the duty of care who fails to obtain it and study it carefully.

FORM ADV

Part I - Page 1

Uniform Application for Investment Adviser Registration

OMB APPROVAL	
OMB Number:	3235-0049
Expires:	April 30, 2000
Estimated average burden hours per response 9.01	

This filing is an: ☐ Initial Application

or an: ☐ Amendment

If this filing is an Amendment:
- Give the Applicant's SEC File Number 801-_____
- Is Applicant now active in business as an Investment Adviser?   Yes ☐   No ☐

WARNING: Failure to complete this Form accurately and keep it current subjects applicant to administrative, civil and criminal penalties.

1. A. Applicant's full name (If sole proprietor, state last, first and middle name):

   B. Name under which business is conducted, if different:

   C. If business name is being amended, give previous name:

2. A. Principal place of business: (Number and Street – Do not use P.O. Box Number)   (City)   (State)   (Zip Code)

   B. Hours business is conducted at this location: from   to   C. Telephone Number at this location: (Area Code)   (Telephone Number)

   D. Mailing address, if different from address given in 2A: (Number and Street or P.O. Box Number)   (City)   (State)   (Zip Code)

   E. Is the address in Item 2A or 2D being amended in this filing? . . . .   Yes ☐   No ☐

   F. On Schedule E give the addresses and telephone numbers of all offices at which applicant's investment advisory business is conducted, other than the one given in Item 2A.

3. A. If books and records required by Section 204 of the Investment Advisers Act of 1940 are kept somewhere other than at the principal place of business given in Item 2A, give the following information (if kept in more than one place, give additional names, addresses and hours of business on Schedule E):

   Name and address of entity where books and records are kept:

   (Number and Street)   (City)   (State)   (Zip Code)

   B. Hours business is conducted at this location: from   to   C. Telephone Number at this location: (Area Code)   (Telephone Number)

EXECUTION

For the purpose of complying with the laws of the State(s) I have marked in Item 7 relating to the giving of investment advice, I hereby certify that the applicant is in compliance with applicable state surety bonding requirements and irrevocably appoint the administrator of each of those State(s), or such other person designated by law, and the successors in such office, my attorney in said State(s) upon whom may be served any notice, process or pleading in any action or proceeding against me arising out of or in connection with the offer or sale of securities or commodities, or out of the violation or alleged violation of the laws of those State(s) and I do hereby consent that any such action or proceeding against me may be commenced in any court of competent jurisdiction and proper venue within said State(s) by service of process upon said appointee with the same effect as if I were a resident in said State(s) and had lawfully been served with process in said State(s).

The undersigned, being first duly sworn, deposes and says that he has executed this Form on behalf of, and with the authority of, said applicant. The undersigned and applicant represent that the information and statements contained herein, including exhibits attached hereto and other information filed herewith, all of which are made a part hereof, are current, true and complete. The undersigned and applicant further represent that to the extent any information previously submitted is not amended, such information is currently accurate and complete.

Date:	Name of Applicant:	By (Signature):

Typed Name and Title:

Subscribed and sworn before me this _____ day of _____ 19 ____

By:

My commission expires _____ County of _____ State of _____

Answer all items.

Potential persons who are to respond to the collection of information contained in this form are not required to respond unless the form displays a currently valid OMB control number.   SEC 1707 (7/97)

FORM ADV
Part I - Page 2

Applicant:	SEC File Number: 801-	Date:

4. A. Persons to contact for further information about this Form: (Name)   (Title)

    B. Mailing Address (Number and Street, City, State, Zip Code):   Area Code and Telephone Number: ( )

5. A. Applicant consents that notice of any proceeding before the Securities and Exchange Commission or a jurisdiction in connection with its investment adviser registration may be given by registered or certified mail or confirmed telegram to: (Last Name) (First Name) (Middle Name)

    B. (Number and Street)   (City)   (State)   (Zip Code)   **6.** Applicant's fiscal year ends: (Month)   (Day)

7. In the box below, give status of applicant's investment adviser registration by indicating:
    "1" for pending   "3" for withdrawn before registration within the last 10 years
    "2" for registered   "4" for previously registered within the last 10 years

Securities and Exchange Commission _____

AL ___	AK ___	AZ ___	AR ___	CA ___	CO ___	CT ___	DE ___	DC ___	FL ___	GA ___	HI ___	ID ___
IL ___	IN ___	IA ___	KS ___	KY ___	LA ___	ME ___	MD ___	MA ___	MI ___	MN ___	MS ___	MO ___
MT ___	NE ___	NV ___	NH ___	NJ ___	NM ___	NY ___	NC ___	ND ___	OH ___	OK ___	OR ___	PA ___
RI ___	SC ___	SD ___	TN ___	TX ___	UT ___	VT ___	VA ___	WA ___	WV ___	WI ___	WY ___	Puerto Rico ___

Other (Specify): _____

8. Applicant is a (check box that applies and complete those items):

A. ☐ CORPORATION - Complete Schedule A.   (1) Date of incorporation (Month, Day, Year):   (2) Jurisdiction where incorporated:

B. ☐ PARTNERSHIP - Complete Schedule B.   (1) Date of establishment (Month, Day, Year):   (2) Current legal address (Number, Street, City, State, Zip Code):

C. ☐ SOLE PROPRIETORSHIP   (1) Date business began (Month, Day, Year):   (2) Current residence address of proprietor: (Number, Street, City, State, Zip Code)   (3) Social Security No.

D. ☐ Other - Specify _____ Complete Schedule C   (1) Date of establishment (Month, Day, Year):   (2) Current legal address (Number, Street, City, State, Zip Code):

9. Is the applicant taking over the business of a registered investment adviser? (If yes, describe the transfer on Schedule E, including the transfer date, and predecessor's full name, IRS employer number and SEC file number) . . . .   Yes ☐   No ☐

10. A. Does any person not named in Item 1A or Schedules A, B, or C, through agreement or otherwise, control the management or policies of applicant? . . . .   Yes ☐   No ☐

    (If yes, state on Schedule E the exact name of each person and describe the basis for the person's control.)

    B. Is the applicant financed by a person not named in Items 1A or Schedule A, B, or C other than by: (1) a public offering under the Securities Act of 1933; (2) credit given in the ordinary course of business by banks, suppliers or others; or (3) a satisfactory subordination agreement under Securities Exchange Act of 1934 Rule 15c3-1 (17 CFR 240.15c3-1)? . . . .   Yes ☐   No ☐

    (If yes, state on Schedule E the exact name of each person and describe the arrangement through which financing is made available, including the amount.)

Answer all items. Complete amended pages in full, circle amended items and file with execution page (page 1).

Applicant:	SEC File Number:	Date:
	801-	

11. Disciplinary questions. Definitions:

- Advisory affiliate — A person named in Items 1A, 10A or Schedules A, B or C; or an individual or firm that directly or indirectly controls or is controlled by the applicant, including any current employee except one performing only clerical, administrative, support or similar functions.

- Investment or investment-related — Pertaining to securities, commodities, banking, insurance, or real estate (including, but not limited to, acting as or being associated with a broker-dealer, investment company, investment adviser, futures sponsor, bank or savings and loan association).

- Involved — Doing an act or aiding, abetting, counseling, commanding, inducing, conspiring with or failing reasonably to supervise another in doing an act.

A. In the past ten years has the applicant or an advisory affiliate been convicted of or pleaded guilty or nolo contendre ("no contest") to:

   (1) a felony or misdemeanor involving:

- investment or an investment-related business
- fraud, false statements, or omissions
- wrongful taking of property or
- bribery, forgery, counterfeiting, or extortion? ....   Yes ☐   No ☐

   (2) any other felony? ....   Yes ☐   No ☐

B. Has any court:

   (1) in the past ten years, enjoined the applicant or an advisory affiliate in connection with any investment-related activity? ....   Yes ☐   No ☐

   (2) ever found that the applicant or an advisory affiliate was involved in a violation of investment-related statutes or regulations? ....   Yes ☐   No ☐

C. Has the U.S. Securities and Exchange Commission or the Commodity Futures Trading Commission ever:

   (1) found the applicant or an advisory affiliate to have made a false statement or omission? ....   Yes ☐   No ☐

   (2) found the applicant or an advisory affiliate to have been involved in a violation of its regulations or statutes?   Yes ☐   No ☐

   (3) found the applicant or an advisory affiliate to have been a cause of an investment-related business having its authorization to do business denied, suspended, revoked, or restricted? ....   Yes ☐   No ☐

   (4) entered an order denying, suspending or revoking the applicant's or an advisory affiliate's registration or otherwise disciplined it by restricting its activities? ....   Yes ☐   No ☐

D. Has any other federal regulatory agency or any state regulatory agency:

   (1) ever found the applicant or an advisory affiliate to have made a false statement or omission or been dishonest, unfair, or unethical? ....   Yes ☐   No ☐

   (2) ever found the applicant or an advisory affiliate to have been involved in a violation of investment regulations or statutes? ....   Yes ☐   No ☐

   (3) ever found the applicant or an advisory affiliate to have been a cause of an investment-related business having its authorization to do business denied, suspended, revoked, or restricted? ....   Yes ☐   No ☐

   (4) in the past ten years, entered an order against the applicant or an advisory affiliate in connection with an investment-related activity? ....   Yes ☐   No ☐

   (5) ever denied, suspended, or revoked the applicant's or an advisory affiliate's registration or license, prevented it from associating with an investment-related business, or otherwise disciplined it by restricting its activities?   Yes ☐   No ☐

   (6) ever revoked or suspended the applicant's or an advisory affiliate's license as an attorney or accountant? ......   Yes ☐   No ☐

Answer all items. Complete amended pages in full, circle amended items and file with execution page (page 1).

Applicant:	SEC File Number: 801-	Date:

E. Has any self-regulatory organization or commodities exchange ever:

    (1) found the applicant or an advisory affiliate to have made a false statement or omission? . . . .   Yes ☐ No ☐

    (2) found the applicant or an advisory affiliate to have been involved in a violation of its rules? . . . .   Yes ☐ No ☐

    (3) found the applicant or an advisory affiliate to have been the cause of an investment-related business having its authorization to do business denied, suspended, revoked, or restricted? . . . .   Yes ☐ No ☐

    (4) disciplined the applicant or an advisory affiliate by expelling or suspending it from membership, by barring or suspending its association with other members, or by otherwise restricting its activities? . . . .   Yes ☐ No ☐

F. Has any foreign government, court, regulatory agency, or exchange ever entered an order against the applicant or an advisory affiliate related to investments or fraud? . . . .   Yes ☐ No ☐

G. Is the applicant or an advisory affiliate now the subject of any proceeding that could result in a 'yes' answer to parts A-F of this item? . . . .   Yes ☐ No ☐

H. Has a bonding company denied, paid out on, or revoked a bond for the applicant? . . . .   Yes ☐ No ☐

I. Does the applicant have any unsatisfied judgments or liens against it? . . . .   Yes ☐ No ☐

J. Has the applicant or an advisory affiliate of the applicant ever been a securities firm or an advisory affiliate of a securities firm that has been declared bankrupt, had a trustee appointed under the Securities Investor Protection Act, or had a direct payment procedure begun? . . . .   Yes ☐ No ☐

K. Has the applicant, or an officer, director or person owning 10% or more of the applicant's securities failed in business, made a compromise with creditors, filed a bankruptcy petition or been declared bankrupt? . . . .   Yes ☐ No ☐

If a 'yes' answer on Item 11 involves:

* an individual, complete a Schedule D for the individual

* a partnership, corporation or other organization, on Schedule E give the following details of any court or regulatory action:
  * the organization and individuals named
  * the title and date of the action
  * the court or body taking the action
  * a description of the action.

12. Individual's Education, Business and Disciplinary Background. Complete a Schedule D for each individual who is:

A. The applicant, named in Part I Item 1A

B. A control person named in Part I Item 10

C. An owner of at least 10% of a class of applicant's equity securities

D. An officer, director, partner, or individual with similar status of applicant, described in Schedule A Item 2a, Schedule B Item 2, or Schedule C Item 2

E. A member of the applicant's investment committee that determines general investment advice to be given to clients

F. If applicant has no investment committee, an individual who determines general investment advice (if more than five, complete for their supervisors only)

G. An individual giving investment advice on behalf of the applicant in the jurisdiction in which this application is filed

H. An individual reporting a 'yes' answer to the disciplinary question, Part I Item 11

Answer all items. Complete amended pages in full, circle amended items and file with execution page (page 1).

Applicant:	SEC File Number: 801-	Date:

13. Does applicant have custody (see definition in instructions) of any advisory client:

    A. funds... Yes ☐   No ☐

    B. securities .... Yes ☐   No ☐

    C. If either answer is yes, the value of those funds and securities at the end of applicant's last fiscal year was:

           (1) ☐ under $100,000   (3) ☐ $1,000,000 to $5,000,000

           (2) ☐ $100,000 to $1,000,000   (4) ☐ Over $5,000,000

---

14. Do any of applicant's related persons have custody (see definition in instructions) of any advisory client:

    A. funds .... Yes ☐   No ☐

    B. securities .... Yes ☐   No ☐

    If either is yes:

    C. is that person a registered broker-dealer qualified to take custody under Section 15 of the Securities Exchange Act of 1934?.. Yes ☐   No ☐

    D. the value of those funds and securities at the end of applicant's last fiscal year was:

           (1) ☐ under $100,000   (3) ☐ $1,000,001 to $5,000,000

           (2) ☐ $100,000 to $1,000,000   (4) ☐ Over $5,000,000

---

15. Does applicant require prepayment of fees of more than $500 per client and more than 6 months in advance? .... Yes ☐   No ☐

---

16. With a few exceptions, the "brochure rule" (Advisers Act Rule 204-3) requires that clients must be given information about the investment adviser. Will applicant be giving clients (other than wrap fee clients to be given Schedule H):

    A. Part II of this Form ADV? .... Yes ☐   No ☐

    B. Another document that includes at least the information contained in Form ADV Part II?.. Yes ☐   No ☐

---

17. A. The number of employees of applicant who perform investment advisory functions (including research, but excluding unrelated functions such as accounting) is: (check only one box)

           (1) ☐ 1 person, part time   (3) ☐ 2-9 persons

           (2) ☐ 1 person primarily involved in   (4) ☐ 10 or more persons
                    providing investment advisory services

    B. The number of clients to whom applicant provided advisory services during the last fiscal year was:

           (1) ☐ 14 or fewer   (4) ☐ 101 to 500

           (2) ☐ 15 to 50   (5) ☐ over 500

           (3) ☐ 51 to 100

Answer all items. Complete amended pages in full, circle amended items and file with execution page (page 1).

Applicant:	SEC File Number: 801-	Date:

18. *Assets Under Management: Discretionary*

Does applicant manage client securities portfolios that receive continuous and regular supervisory or management services on a discretionary basis? ....   Yes ☐   No ☐

If yes, at the end of applicant's last fiscal year:

    A. these securities portfolios numbered _____ .

    B. these securities portfolios, in aggregate market value, totaled $ _____ .00 (to nearest dollar)

Determine: (i) whether an account is a "securities portfolio"; (ii) whether a securities portfolio receives "continuous and regular supervisory or management services"; and (iii) the aggregate market value of such a securities portfolio, in accordance with Instruction 7 of Schedule I to Form ADV. Items 18(B) and 19(B) should total the response (if any) to Part II of Schedule I.

19. *Assets Under Management: Non-Discretionary*

Does applicant manage or supervise client securities portfolios that receive continuous and regular supervisory or management services on a non-discretionary basis? ....   Yes ☐   No ☐

If yes, at the end of applicant's last fiscal year:

    A. these securities portfolios numbered _____ .

    B. these securities portfolios, in aggregate market value, totaled $ _____ .00 (to nearest dollar)

Determine: (i) whether an account is a "securities portfolio"; (ii) whether a securities portfolio receives "continuous and regular supervisory or management services"; and (iii) the aggregate market value of such a securities portfolio, in accordance with Instruction 7 of Schedule I to Form ADV. Items 18(B) and 19(B) should total the response (if any) to Part II of Schedule I.

20. Does applicant hold itself out as providing financial planning or some similarly termed services to clients? ....   Yes ☐   No ☐

If yes, during the last fiscal year applicant provided financial planning services to clients:

  A. who numbered:

    (1) ☐ 14 or fewer   (4) ☐ 101 to 500

    (2) ☐ 15 to 50   (5) ☐ over 500

    (3) ☐ 51 to 100

  B. whose investments in financial products based on those services totaled:

    (1) ☐ under $100,000   (3) ☐ $1,000,001 to $5,000,000

    (2) ☐ $100,000 to $1,000,000   (4) ☐ over $5,000,000

21. Did applicant recommend securities to clients during its last fiscal year in which the applicant acted (itself or through a related person) as an underwriter, general or managing partner, or offeree representative, or had any ownership or sales interest (other than the receipt of normal and customary sales commissions as a broker or brokers representative)? ....   Yes ☐   No ☐

If yes, the approximate value of securities so recommended during its last fiscal year is:

A. ☐ Under $50,000   C. ☐ $250,001 to $1,000,000

B. ☐ $50,000 to $250,000   D. ☐ over $1,000,000

22. Attach to this Form any financial statements required by the jurisdiction in which applicant is filing, other than the balance sheet required by Part II item 14.

Answer all items. Complete amended pages in full, circle amended items and file with execution page (page 1).

OMB APPROVAL	
OMB Number:	3235-0049
Expires:	April 30, 2000
Estimated average burden hours per response 9.01	

Name of Investment Adviser:

Address:	(Number and Street)	(City)	(State)	(Zip Code)	Area Code:	Telephone Number: ( )

This part of Form ADV gives information about the investment adviser and its business for the use of clients. The information has not been approved or verified by any governmental authority.

Table of Contents

(Schedules A, B, C, D, and E are included with Part I of this Form, for the use of regulatory bodies, and are not distributed to clients.)

Potential persons who are to respond to the collection of information contained in this form are not required to respond unless the form displays a currently valid OMB control number.

Applicant:	SEC File Number: 801-	Date:

Definitions for Part II

Related person — Any officer, director or partner of applicant or any person directly or indirectly controlling, controlled by, or under common control with the applicant, including any non-clerical, non-ministerial employee.

Investment Supervisory Services — Giving continuous investment advice to a client (or making investments for the client) based on the individual needs of the client. Individual needs include, for example, the nature of other client assets and the client's personal and family obligations.

---

1. **A. Advisory Services and Fees.** (check the applicable boxes)   For each type of service provided, state the approximate % of total advisory billings from that service. (See instruction below.)

    Applicant:

    ☐ (1) Provides investment supervisory services . . . . _____ %
    ☐ (2) Manages investment advisory accounts not involving investment supervisory services . . . . _____ %
    ☐ (3) Furnishes investment advice through consultations not included in either service described above . . . . . _____ %
    ☐ (4) Issues periodicals about securities by subscription . . . . _____ %
    ☐ (5) Issues special reports about securities not included in any service described above . . . . _____ %
    ☐ (6) Issues, not as part of any service described above, any charts, graphs, formulas, or other devices which clients may use to evaluate securities . . . . _____ %
    ☐ (7) On more than an occasional basis, furnishes advice to clients on matters not involving securities . . . . . _____ %
    ☐ (8) Provides a timing service . . . . _____ %
    ☐ (9) Furnishes advice about securities in any manner not described above . . . . _____ %

    (Percentages should be based on applicant's last fiscal year. If applicant has not completed its first fiscal year, provide estimates of advisory billings for that year and state that the percentages are estimates.)

	Yes	No
B. Does applicant call any of the services it checked above financial planning or some similar term?	☐	☐

    C. Applicant offers investment advisory services for: (check all that apply)

    ☐ (1) A percentage of assets under management   ☐ (4) Subscription fees
    ☐ (2) Hourly charges   ☐ (5) Commissions
    ☐ (3) Fixed fees (not including subscription fees)   ☐ (6) Other

---

    D. For each checked box in A above, describe on Schedule F:

    • the services provided, including the name of any publication or report issued by the adviser on a subscription basis or for a fee

    • applicant's basic fee schedule, how fees are charged and whether its fees are negotiable

    • when compensation is payable, and if compensation is payable before service is provided, how a client may get a refund or may terminate an investment advisory contract before its expiration date

---

2. **Types of Clients** — Applicant generally provides investment advice to: (check those that apply)

    ☐ A. Individuals   ☐ E. Trusts, estates, or charitable organizations

    ☐ B. Banks or thrift institutions   ☐ F. Corporations or business entities other than those listed above

    ☐ C. Investment companies
                                                    ☐ G. Other (describe on Schedule F)
    ☐ D. Pension and profit sharing plans

Answer all items. Complete amended pages in full, circle amended items and file with execution page (page 1).

Applicant:	SEC File Number: 801-	Date:

3. **Types of Investments.** Applicant offers advice on the following: (check those that apply)

A. Equity Securities
- ☐ (1) exchange-listed securities
- ☐ (2) securities traded over-the-counter
- ☐ (3) foreign issuers

☐ B. Warrants

☐ C. Corporate debt securities
   (other than commercial paper)

☐ D. Commercial paper

☐ E. Certificates of deposit

☐ F. Municipal securities

G. Investment company securities:
- ☐ (1) variable life insurance
- ☐ (2) variable annuities
- ☐ (3) mutual fund shares

☐ H. United States government securities

I. Options contracts on:
- ☐ (1) securities
- ☐ (2) commodities

J. Futures contracts on:
- ☐ (1) tangibles
- ☐ (2) intangibles

K. Interests in partnerships investing in:
- ☐ (1) real estate
- ☐ (2) oil and gas interests
- ☐ (3) other (explain on Schedule F)

☐ L. Other (explain on Schedule F)

4. **Methods of Analysis, Sources of Information, and Investment Strategies.**

A. Applicant's security analysis methods include: (check those that apply)

- (1) ☐ Charting
- (2) ☐ Fundamental
- (3) ☐ Technical
- (4) ☐ Cyclical
- (5) ☐ Other (explain on Schedule F)

B. The main sources of information applicant uses include: (check those that apply)

- (1) ☐ Financial newspapers and magazines
- (2) ☐ Inspections of corporate activities
- (3) ☐ Research materials prepared by others
- (4) ☐ Corporate rating services
- (5) ☐ Timing services
- (6) ☐ Annual reports, prospectuses, filings with the Securities and Exchange Commission
- (7) ☐ Company press releases
- (8) ☐ Other (explain on Schedule F)

C. The investment strategies used to implement any investment advice given to clients include: (check those that apply)

- (1) ☐ Long term purchases (securities held at least a year)
- (2) ☐ Short term purchases (securities sold within a year)
- (3) ☐ Trading (securities sold within 30 days)
- (4) ☐ Short sales
- (5) ☐ Margin transactions
- (6) ☐ Option writing, including covered options, uncovered options or spreading strategies
- (7) ☐ Other (explain on Schedule F)

Answer all items. Complete amended pages in full, circle amended items and file with execution page (page 1).

Applicant:	SEC File Number: 801-	Date:

5.   Education and Business Standards.

Are there any general standards of education or business experience that applicant requires of those involved in determining or giving investment advice to clients? . . . .

Yes ☐   No ☐

(If yes, describe these standards on Schedule F.)

6.   Education and Business Background.

For:

- each member of the investment committee or group that determines general investment advice to be given to clients, or

- if the applicant has no investment committee or group, each individual who determines general investment advice given to clients (if more than five, respond only for their supervisors)

- each principal executive officer of applicant or each person with similar status or performing similar functions.

On Schedule F, give the:

- name
- year of birth
- formal education after high school
- business background for the preceding five years

7.   Other Business Activities. (check those that apply)

☐   A.   Applicant is actively engaged in a business other than giving investment advice.

☐   B.   Applicant sells products or services other than investment advice to clients.

☐   C.   The principal business of applicant or its principal executive officers involves something other than providing investment advice.

(For each checked box describe the other activities, including the time spent on them, on Schedule F.)

8.   Other Financial Industry Activities or Affiliations. (check those that apply)

☐   A.   Applicant is registered (or has an application pending) as a securities broker-dealer.

☐   B.   Applicant is registered (or has an application pending) as a futures commission merchant, commodity pool operator or commodity trading adviser.

C.   Applicant has arrangements that are material to its advisory business or its clients with a related person who is a:

☐   (1) broker-dealer

☐   (2) investment company

☐   (3) other investment adviser

☐   (4) financial planning firm

☐   (5) commodity pool operator. commodity trading adviser or futures commission merchant

☐   (6) banking or thrift institution

☐   (7) accounting firm

☐   (8) law firm

☐   (9) insurance company or agency

☐   (10) pension consultant

☐   (11) real estate broker or dealer

☐   (12) entity that creates or packages limited partnerships

(For each checked box in C, on Schedule F identify the related person and describe the relationship and the arrangements.)

D.   Is applicant or a related person a general partner in any partnership in which clients are solicited to invest? . . . .

Yes ☐   No ☐

(If yes, describe on Schedule F the partnerships and what they invest in.)

Answer all items. Complete amended pages in full, circle amended items and file with execution page (page 1).

Applicant:	SEC File Number: 801-	Date:

9. **Participation or Interest in Client Transactions.**

Applicant or a related person: (check those that apply)

☐ A. As principal, buys securities for itself from or sells securities it owns to any client.

☐ B. As broker or agent effects securities transactions for compensation for any client.

☐ C. As broker or agent for any person other than a client effects transactions in which client securities are sold to or bought from a brokerage customer.

☐ D. Recommends to clients that they buy or sell securities or investment products in which the applicant or a related person has some financial interest.

☐ E. Buys or sells for itself securities that it also recommends to clients.

(For each box checked, describe on Schedule F when the applicant or a related person engages in these transactions and what restrictions, internal procedures, or disclosures are used for conflicts of interest in those transactions.)

10. **Conditions for Managing Accounts.** Does the applicant provide investment supervisory services, manage investment advisory accounts or hold itself out as providing financial planning or some similarly termed services *and* impose a minimum dollar value of assets or other conditions for starting or maintaining an account? . . . .

Yes ☐   No ☐

(If yes, describe on Schedule F.)

11. **Review of Accounts.** If applicant provides investment supervisory services, manages investment advisory accounts, or holds itself out as providing financial planning or some similarly termed services:

A. Describe below the reviews and reviewers of the accounts. **For reviews,** include their frequency, different levels, and triggering factors. **For reviewers,** include the number of reviewers, their titles and functions, instructions they receive from applicant on performing reviews, and number of accounts assigned each.

B. Describe below the nature and frequency of regular reports to clients on their accounts.

Answer all items. Complete amended pages in full, circle amended items and file with execution page (page 1).

Applicant:	SEC File Number: 801-	Date:

12. Investment or Brokerage Discretion.

   A. Does applicant or any related person have authority to determine, without obtaining specific client consent, the:

       (1) securities to be bought or sold? . . . .

       (2) amount of the securities to be bought or sold? . . . .

       (3) broker or dealer to be used? . . . .

       (4) commission rates paid? . . . .

   B. Does applicant or a related person suggest brokers to clients? . . . .

       For each yes answer to A describe on Schedule F any limitations on the authority. For each yes to A(3), A(4) or B, describe on Schedule F the factors considered in selecting brokers and determining the reasonableness of their commissions. If the value of products, research and services given to the applicant or a related person is a factor, describe:

     • the products, research and services

     • whether clients may pay commissions higher than those obtainable from other brokers in return for those products and services

     • whether research is used to service all of applicant's accounts or just those accounts paying for it; and

     • any procedures the applicant used during the last fiscal year to direct client transactions to a particular broker in return for products and research services received.

13. Additional Compensation.

   Does the applicant or a related person have any arrangements, oral or in writing, where it:

   A. is paid cash by or receives some economic benefit (including commissions, equipment or non-research services) from a non-client in connection with giving advice to clients?. . . . .

   B. directly or indirectly compensates any person for client referrals? . . . .

                        (For each yes, describe the arrangements on Schedule F.

14. Balance Sheet. Applicant must provide a balance sheet for the most recent fiscal year on Schedule G if applicant:

     • has custody of client funds or securities; or

     • requires prepayment of more than $500 in fees per client and 6 or more months in advance

       Has applicant provided a Schedule G balance sheet? . . . .

Answer all items. Complete amended pages in full, circle amended items and file with execution page (page 1).

Schedule A of Form ADV FOR CORPORATIONS	Applicant:		SEC File Number: 801-	Date:	Official Use

1. This Schedule requests information on the owners and executive officers of the applicant.

2. Please complete for:

   (a) each Chief Executive Officer, Chief Financial Officer, Chief Operations Officer, Chief Legal Officer, Chief Compliance Officer, director, and individuals with similar status or functions, and

   (b) every person who is directly, or indirectly through intermediaries, the beneficial owner of 5% or more of any class of equity security of the applicant.

3. If a person covered by 2(b) above owns applicant indirectly through intermediaries, list all intermediaries and below them, if they are not subject to Sections 12 or 15(d) of the Securities Exchange Act of 1934 but are:

   (a) corporations, give their shareholders who own 5% or more of a class of equity security, or

   (b) partnerships, give their general partners or any limited and special partners who have contributed 5% or more of the partnership's capital.

4. If the intermediary's shareholders or partners listed under 3 above are not individuals, continue up the chain of ownership listing their 5% shareholders, general partners, and 5% limited or special partners until individuals are listed.

5. Ownership codes are: NA - 0   up to 5%   B - 10% up to 25%   D - 50% up to 75%
   A - 5% up to 10%   C - 25% up to 50%   E - 75% up to 100%

6. Asterisk (*) names reporting a change in title, status, stock ownership or partnership interest or control. Double asterisk (**) names new on this filing.

7. Check "Control Person" column if person has "control" as defined in the instructions to this Form.

FULL NAME			Beginning Date		Title or Status	Owner-ship Code	Control Person	CRD No., or, if none Social Security Number	OFFICIAL USE ONLY
Last	First	Middle	Month	Year					

List below names reported on the most recent previous filing under this item that are being DELETED:

FULL NAME			Ending Date		CRD. No., or, if none Social Security Number
Last	First	Middle	Month	Year	

Complete amended pages in full, circle amended items and file with execution page (page 1).

251

<table>
<tr><td rowspan="3">Schedule B of
Form ADV
FOR PARTNERSHIPS</td><td colspan="2">Applicant:</td><td>SEC File Number:
801-</td><td>Date:</td><td>Official Use</td></tr>
</table>

Schedule B of **Form ADV** **FOR PARTNERSHIPS**	Applicant:	SEC File Number: 801-	Date:	Official Use

(Answers for Form ADV Part I Item 8.)

1. This Schedule requests information on the owners and partners of the applicant.

2. Please complete for all general partners and with respect to limited and special partners all those who have contributed directly or indirectly through intermediaries, 5% or more of the partnership's capital.

3. If a person owns applicant indirectly through intermediaries, list all intermediaries and below them, if they are not subject to Sections 12 or 15(d) of the Securities Exchange Act of 1934 but are:

    (a) corporations, give their shareholders who own 5% or more of a class of equity security, or

    (b) partnerships, give their general partners or any limited and special partners who have contributed 5% or more of the partnership's capital.

4. If the intermediary's shareholders or partners listed under 3 above are not individuals, continue up the chain of ownership listing their 5% shareholders, general partners, and 5% limited or special partners until individuals are listed.

5. Ownership codes are: NA - 0 up to 5% B - 10% up to 25% D - 50% up to 75%
    A - 5% up to 10% C - 25% up to 50% E - 75% up to 100%

6. Asterisk (*) names reporting a change in title, status, stock ownership or partnership interest or control. Double asterisk (**) names new on this filing.

7. Check "Control Person" column if person has "control" as defined in the instructions to this Form.

FULL NAME			Beginning Date		Title or Status	Owner-ship Code	Control Person	CRD No., or, if none Social Security Number	OFFICIAL USE ONLY
Last	First	Middle	Month	Year					

List below names reported on the most recent previous filing under this item that are being DELETED:

FULL NAME			Ending Date		CRD No., or, if none Social Security Number
Last	First	Middle	Month	Year	

Complete amended pages in full, circle amended items and file with execution page (page 1).

Glossary

Acceptance clause The clause in a trust agreement by which a trustee accepts his responsibility as trustee.

Accounting A detailed report to the trust beneficiaries by a trustee of his stewardship, also used to discharge the trustee.

Accrual basis Valuation based on accrual, not cash. Thus, dividends are included on the ex-dividend date rather than the payment date.

Accumulate Wall Street expression for buying on a large scale over time, typically by an institution. "Accumulation" of a stock is said to occur if a number of institutions are gradually adding to their holdings.

Accumulations In discretionary trusts, income retained by the trustee rather than paid out.

Acknowledgment Part of a trust agreement, generally completed by a notary public and located on the signature page, in which the parties confirm that their signatures are true.

Active cash Seeking the best rate on short-term funds.

Active duration Lengthening a fixed-income portfolio in the expectation of lower interest rates or vice versa.

Additions Assets transferred to a trust after the initial funding.

Administrative powers The trustee's powers, expressed or implied, to operate the trust, as distinct from disposing of the beneficial interest. (See **dispositive power**.)

Advance-decline ratio A useful barometer of the underlying condition of the market. Toward the end of a long upward sweep, speculative interest is concentrated on the small number of stocks that are still struggling forward while, masked by the activity of those few, the rest of the market fades. As the peak nears, the number of stocks going up becomes less and less. If each day you plot a graph of the number of stocks that advanced minus the number of stocks that declined, that line will normally turn down months before the Dow does.

Aggressive Implies a concentrated portfolio holding smaller capitalization stocks than the general market, often with higher price/earnings and lower yields, together with low reserves. Often implies unusual volatility.

AIMR A standard performance presentation system. For information call 804-980-3547 or go to http://www.aimr.org.

Alpha Portfolio return above or below the general market return, taking account of volatility.

Alternative investments Hedge funds, venture capital pools, options and other derivatives, real estate, and other non-stock or -bond market securities.

American Depositary Receipt (ADR) Certificate which can be traded on a U.S. market, issued by a U.S. bank representing its holding abroad of a foreign stock. The market prices may not correspond: ten shares of a $2 German stock may be consolidated into a $20 ADR.

Arithmetic return The entire return divided, without compounding, by the number of periods. For instance, if a stock doubles in ten years, the arithmetic return would be 10 percent per annum, while the **compound return** would be 7 percent.

Asking price A market-maker always indicates a "spread" for a stock (e.g., 25 bid - 25¼ offered). If you want to sell, he offers the bid price; if you want to buy, he sells at his asking price.

Asset allocation Maneuvering among asset classes (e.g., stocks versus bonds, large capitalization versus small capitalization, domestic versus foreign securities, and developed versus emerging markets).

Balanced fund A mixture of stocks and bonds.

Basic fee The straight asset-based management fee, on top of which may be added a performance fee.

Basis point A hundredth of a percent; thus 75 basis points equals three-quarters of 1 percentage point.

Benchmark The standard—typically an average—against which the investment performance in a given category can be measured (e.g., the S&P 500 for U.S. equities).

Beneficiaries; beneficial interests Those who receive trust income are generally known as "income beneficiaries," and those who receive the trust principal at its termination as **remaindermen**.

Beta An unreliable measure of the volatility of a stock as compared with the general averages. A beta of 1.0 would mean that a stock moves hand in hand with the general market. But betas can be computed in different ways, and they change anyway. The market is measured by indexes with different characteristics.

Bigger-fool theory A risky investment technique, but effective when practiced by a master speculator. It consists of applying to the investing public the type of calculation made by a skillful politician. Just as the truth is often unpalatable to the electorate and unsound policies are often popular for a while, so too the reaction of the public to a plausible story about a company is sometimes easier to foresee than how the business itself will make out. The investor is not certain he is buying a solid value, but he foresees a desire by less-informed investors —the "bigger fools"—to take it off his hands when the time comes.

Block A large stock transaction (e.g., ten thousand shares or more).

Blue chip A large, stable, well-known, widely held, seasoned company with a strong financial position, usually paying a reasonable dividend.

Boilerplate The standard language in a legal document, as distinct from that specific to the security or matter in question.

Book value Book value is based on accounting principles, not on appraised value of assets. From the cost of a company's assets one deducts appreciation and debt. Since assets may increase in real value because of inflation or other factors, whereas for balance sheet purposes they are depreciated, the book value of a good company may well be lower than its real value. (See **Tobin's Q**.) For a company with obsolete equipment, both may be meaningless. "Hard book" means that all doubtful assets have been written down. The book value of, for example, the S&P 500 means less, as the underlying companies are increasingly in service industries.

On a securities portfolio appraisal, cost may be called book value.

Bottom-up Developing a portfolio by focusing on individual securities.

Breakout When a stock penetrates the highest price previously recorded; see **free wheeling**.

Capitalization-weighted An index that weighs its components according to their market capitalization, instead of giving them equal weight; manager performance calculated weighting the size of the portfolios managed.

Care One of the three components of the standard of prudence governing trustees; the duty to inquire and investigate before taking action.

Cash sweep When the excess cash in an account is automatically placed in a money fund at specified intervals.

Caution One of the three components of the standard of prudence governing trustees; avoidance of undue risk and attentiveness to the protection of trust property.

CBOE Chicago Board of Options Exchange.

Certificate of deposit An unsecured evidence of indebtedness of a bank, which may be sold to others. Usually with a face value of $100,000 or more and bearing interest below the prime rate.

Cestui que trust (Archaic) The beneficiary of a trust.

Chartist A variety of technician who bases his forecasting on the formations traced by stock prices: "rounding bottoms," "head and shoulders tops," "pennants," and so forth. All but impossible to practice effectively.

Closed-end fund An investment company that does not sell or redeem its own shares.

Commercial paper Evidence of short-term unsecured corporate indebtedness.

Commingled fund Typically, an investment pool run by a bank, in which participation is represented by accounting units rather than shares.

Commission recapture Credit for brokerage generated is then applied to such services as custody and appraisal.

Common trust funds Found only in bank trust companies, and authorized by federal or state law. Used primarily to invest small individual trusts.

Complex trusts A federal income tax term governing trusts that authorize discretionary power over the payment of current or accumulated trust income.

Compound return In each period (e.g., monthly, quarterly, or annually), the percentage change is applied to the latest valuation, not the original starting valuation. See **arithmetic return**.

Contingent interest An interest in a trust whose enjoyment is not absolute or vested, but rather dependent on a condition being met.

Contrarian investing Seeking stocks, industries, countries, and styles that are out of vogue at the moment; that is, good investing, since investment opportunity is the difference between the reality and the perception.

Convertible A bond or preferred stock that offers the investor the right to convert his holding into common stock under set terms.

Core bond strategy Seeks to create a fixed-income portfolio that approximates a bond index.

Core equity strategy Seeks to create a stock portfolio that approximates a stock index.

Core international Seeks to create a portfolio that approximates markets in developed countries, often as measured by the Morgan Stanley International EAFF Index.

Corporate trustee A bank or trust company having federal or state authority to serve as a trustee.

Corpus The property owned by a trust.

Correction A smaller movement against the major "primary" trend of the market. A **secondary reaction**.

Correlation See **covariance**.

Coupon The interest rate on a bond, expressed as a percentage of its face (not market) value. At one time bonds (and indeed stocks) contained coupons resembling postage stamps, which one "clipped" or cut periodically and presented for payment of interest (or dividends).

Covariance The degree to which two asset classes (e.g., the U.S. market and a foreign market) move closely together.

Creator (of a trust) See **settlor**.

Crummey power/notice The power of a trust beneficiary, given by the trust agreement, to withdraw additions made to a trust by a grantor. Enables such additions to qualify for the federal gift tax annual exclusion. Trustees generally have responsibility to notify a Crummey Power holder of such an addition. See **gift tax exclusion trusts**.

Current yield The yield of a bond, expressed as a percentage of its market price (not face value). The lower the market price of a bond with a given coupon, the higher the current yield, and vice versa.

Custodians Agents who hold property in safekeeping for others, usually without inherent investment management responsibility.

Cyclicals Some industries are perennially subject to the vagaries of the business cycle: mining, steel, construction, automobiles, chemicals, machine tools, and the like. It is impossible to get away from the cyclical effect in business, just as there is always alternation between good and bad weather, so a cyclical company will have an irregular earnings pattern, and usually an irregular stock price pattern too.

Declaration of trust Announcement of the creation of a trust, usually through a written trust agreement; sometimes used to describe a "self-declared" trust, where the grantor also serves as the trustee of a revocable trust.

Deed of trust The written instrument or document incorporating the terms of a trust relationship.

Defensive strategy In fixed-income investments, holding short maturities, so that the portfolio will not fluctuate sharply as interest rates change. In equity investment, avoiding an **aggressive** strategy (*q.v.*), while maintaining comfortable reserves.

Defined benefit plan A retirement plan that specifies the amount an employee collects after different periods of employment.

Defined contribution plan A retirement plan with benefits based on the earnings of the contributions made, taking account of the length of employment.

Delegation of powers The act of entrusting to another a duty or responsibility.

Delta The sensitivity of an option's price to that of the underlying security.

Derivative A security represents a claim on a thing. A derivative represents a claim on a security or invented category: a put or call on a stock, bond, index, or whatever. They carry enormous leverage, and corresponding potential for gain or loss.

Descendants The direct parental line, including children, grandchildren, great-grandchildren, and so on.

Directed brokerage A manager is asked to direct business to a specified broker, usually to pay for services.

Discretionary powers Powers giving a trustee the choice of taking or not taking certain actions, such as the payment of trust income or principal to the beneficiaries, or the allocation of receipts or expenses.

Discretionary trusts Trusts giving the trustee the disposition over trust income or principal during the term of the trust, but usually not at its termination.

Dispositive power The power, always expressed in the trust instrument, to dispose of trust's income and principal. (See **administrative powers**.)

Distribution (phase) Stocks pass from a few large investors, typically institutional, to many smaller ones; usually amid public excitement and effervescent prices.

Dividend yield The yield of a stock, expressed as a percentage of its market price.

Domicile A trust's domicile, sometimes called its "situs," is generally, but not always, the state whose law governs the trust at its inception. See also **situs of trust**.

Dow Jones Industrial Average (**DJI** or **DJIA**) A price-weighted average of thirty industrial companies.

Dow theory Crudely, the view that market currents tend to move in major and minor trends. A major trend in the DJI should be "confirmed" by the transportation average, on the reasoning that authentically improved business will be reflected in higher movement of goods, and thus better profits of carriers.

Down tick A stock trade at a lower price than the last previous transaction.

Duration The average maturity of a bond. The longer the duration, the more sensitive will be the price to interest rate changes.

Earnings yield The reciprocal of the price-earnings ratio. For instance, a P/E of twenty times is an earnings yield of 5 percent.

Economic Value Added (**EVA**) A company's record of profit over the cost of capital: a rightly popular management test.

Efficient Market Hypothesis Crudely, the belief that since all information about stocks is available, their current market price represents their true value. If this were true, certain investors would not achieve consistently superior results, which they do, and since all information about a chess game is available to both opponents, there should not be consistently superior players. All information is never known, judgment is unevenly distributed, and decision making is imperfectly organized and moved by great tides of emotion.

Emerging markets Often, countries so defined by the International Finance Corporation (IFC), based on their per capita income.

Employee Retirement Income Security Act (**ERISA**) Governs most private pension and benefit plans.

Employee stock ownership plan (**ESOP**) An arrangement under which employees of a company borrow to buy the company's own stock. Both the lender and the company enjoy tax advantages.

Equal weighted An index (e.g., the Value Line Index) that gives equal weight to all stocks regardless of their market capitalization; manager performance calculated without weighting the size of the portfolios managed.

Equilibrium spending rate The reasonable withdrawal rate from an endowment to reflect long-term portfolio growth minus an allowance for cost increases.

Equities Another name for shares. The capitalization of a company consists of "equity"—or ownership—represented by common or preferred shares (stock), and debt, represented by bonds, notes, and the like. (In England, "corporation stock" means municipal bonds, incidentally.)

Eurodollars Dollar claims reloaned in Europe without passing through the U.S. banking system.

Exculpatory clause A provision in a trust agreement that frees a trustee from liability for fault or a breach in the discharge of fiduciary duty.

Executor The legal representative of a person who dies with a will.

Exercising price The price at which the owner of an option has the right to buy or sell the underlying stock. (Also called the **striking price**.)

Expectancy A trust beneficiary income or principal to be paid out in the future.

Expected duration The average time of expected future principal and interest flows.

Express powers Explicit authorities of a trustee, specified in a trust agreement and state law. See also **implied powers**.

Federal estate tax A transfer tax imposed on the transfer of property by an individual at death.

Federal gift tax A transfer tax imposed on the transfer of property by an individual during life.

Fiduciary relationship An arrangement under which a person (the fiduciary) has a duty to act for another's benefit (the beneficiary).

Final accounting A written report by a trustee of all income and principal transactions of a trust from inception of the trust, or from the last accounting date, through the termination of the trust.

Free wheeling When a stock has penetrated its previous upper resistance level.

Fulcrum fee A performance fee structure that reduces the basic fee if performance falls below the benchmark, as well as rewarding returns above the benchmark.

Fundamentalist Believes that the best investment results are achieved by studying the specific facts about a company, its industry, and the economy in general, as distinct from considering cycles in investment psychology or divining the future of the market by stock patterns.

Future interests In trusts, a future interest can be a share of the trust's future income, or of the principal at the trust's termination.

Gamma How a security's price changes affect an option's **delta** (*q.v.*). Low for small price changes and high for large ones.

Gap If a stock trades at 20 at the close on Tuesday and begins trading on Wednesday morning at 21, a one-point gap has opened.

Generation-skipping transfers Generally, transfers of property by gift or by will, outright or in trust, to persons who are more than one generation below that of the donor or testator, such as grandchildren, great-grandchildren, and so on.

Gift tax exclusion trusts Inter vivos trusts that qualify for the "annual exclusion" from the federal gift tax, currently limited to $10,000 per donee or donee trust in each calendar year, or $20,000 if a spouse consents to treat the gift as made by both spouses. The annual exclusion is allowed only for "present interests," not for "future interests."

Glamor (or glamour) stock A stock that is exciting high public interest at the moment. Usually a risky purchase.

Global Of a fund or portfolio, invested both in the United States and abroad.

Go-go Said of funds or managers who trade overactively in a booming market.

Good buying Said when a stock is being **accumulated** (*q.v.*) by strong, informed buyers.

Governing law The state law that controls the legal matters of the trust, usually identified by a specific provision in the trust agreement.

Grantor See **settlor**.

Growth at a reasonable price (GARP) A modified growth strategy, giving somewhat less weight to future expectations, and thus implying moderate price-earnings ratios.

Growth investing Emphasizes the future over apparent immediate undervaluation. Thus, usually implies buying companies with higher than average price-earnings ratios and lower dividend yields.

Guaranteed investment contract (GIC) Issued by an insurance company to provide a specific investment return.

Hard dollars Cash payment for services, as distinct from through brokerage commissions.

Head and shoulders (top or bottom) The formation said to exist when a stock has rebounded three times from a **resistance level** (*q.v.*).

Hedge Offsetting investment risk by short sales, put options, etc.

Hedge fund An investing partnership that invests either on the long side or on the short side of the market, or both at once. The theory is that it will be on the long side when the market is going up and on the short side when it is going down. Another theory is that if the manager has no opinion on the overall market he can be long the stocks he likes and short the stocks he dislikes, and so profit in both directions. In practice, few managers perform this feat successfully. Another meaning—acutally, a misnomer—is a fund that does not in fact necessarily hedge, but speculates actively, using margin and/or derivatives. Hedge funds are most numerous, and often most exposed on the long side, at tops, and thus often lose investors more money than they make. Their popularity is, in fact, a bull market indicator.

High yield See **junk bonds**.

Hot issue A newly issued stock that is in strong demand; often it will go to a premium over its original issue price.

Implied powers Powers of a trustee that are not expressed by terms of reference in a trust agreement, or state or court-made law, but derive from those expressed powers.

Income beneficiary A person entitled to all or a share of the income of a trust.

Income commissions The compensation of a trustee that is based on the income of a trust.

Income of trust Dividends, interest, rents, and the like produced by the principal of a trust. The accounting and the taxable income of a trust are different concepts, not necessarily identical.

Indenture The text of a bond.

Index fund A portfolio designed to replicate the performance of an index.

Individual trustee A person serving as a trustee, as distinguished from a corporate or institutional trustee.

Inherent power An authority to act that is an essential part of a trustee's responsibility. See i**mplied powers**.

Initial public offering (IPO) The first time a company's stock is offered in the market. Since this involves considerable fanfare, it is often at a high price.

Institution A retirement fund, bank, investment company, investment advisor, insurance company, or other large pool of investment buying power.

Insurance trust A trust that owns a life insurance policy as part of its corpus.

Intangible property Common stocks, bonds, and other securities representing ownership interest, rather than the physical thing itself (e.g., a home).

Intermediate Of bonds, usually five to seven years' maturity.

International Of a fund or portfolio, invested outside the United States. Once, there was a gain in rate of return to be achieved by the very fact of investing abroad. This is no longer evident.

Intermediate accounting A written report by a trustee of all transactions of a trust covering a period of time that does not end with the termination of the trust. See **final accounting**.

Inter vivos trust A trust established by a person during life, rather than by a will.

In the money Said of an option when the underlying stock is selling for more than the exercising price.

Invasion of principal Paying out a portion of the principal of a trust to a beneficiary before the termination of a trust.

Investing Buying an asset, such as a bond, corporate stock, rental property, or farm, with reasonably determinable underlying earnings.

Investment company (also mutual fund) A company registered under the Investment Company Act of 1930, which provides that in the proper circumstances a company whose only activity is investing need not pay corporate tax. They are closely supervised by the SEC.

If an investment company continuously offers its stock to the public and also redeems it from shareholders who wish to sell, it is said to be open-ended.

If it has a fixed capitalization, it is said to be closed-ended.

Investment grade Bonds rated AAA to BBB.

Irrevocable trusts A trust that cannot be revoked. See **revocable trusts, testamentary trusts**.

Issue The descendants in any degree from a common ancestor.

Junk bonds Below **investment grade** (BBB).

Kicker See **warrant**. Typically, an equity bonus to "sweeten" a bond deal.

Large capitalization Companies with a market capitalization of over $10 billion.

Letter stock (or investment letter stock) "Sophisticated" buyers may buy stock directly from a company without the benefit of a prospectus or a public issue, at a discount from the quoted market price. The SEC requires that the buyer give the seller a letter stating that the unregistered stock is being bought for investment and will be held for a considerable period of time, usually about two years, to indicate *bona fides*. The situation of the company can change drastically during the period, leaving the buyer stuck. Letter stock is often popular during the euphoric period of a market rise.

Leverage Leverage (in England "gearing") is of two sorts: financial and sales. If a company is capitalized half in stock and half in bonds, for instance, a 10 percent change in profits will produce roughly a 20 percent change in earnings per share.

Sales leverage is greatest when a company is operating near the break-even point, so that a small change in sales produces a larger change in profits.

Leveraged buyout (LBO) When an investor or group borrows money, usually on the security of a company's own assets, to take control of it, usually expecting to sell assets to reduce this debt.

Life beneficiary The beneficiary who is entitled to the income benefits of a trust during his or her life.

Life tenant A life beneficiary of a trust.

Liquidity The extent to which a stock trades widely in the market, and can thus be purchased or sold without excessively influencing the price. Also, a company's net asset position, particularly in cash or cash equivalents.

Living trust A trust created during the life of the person creating the trust. See also **inter vivos trust**.

Load A mutual fund's selling commission.

Long To be long a stock simply means that you own it.

Management buyout An **LBO** (*q.v.*), led by insiders.

Mandatory powers Powers that a trustee must exercise in accordance with the terms of the trust agreement or local law. See **discretionary powers**.

Margin The percentage of the market price that an investor must have in underlying equity to hold the stock at a brokerage house or bank. From time to time it may be raised to discourage speculation or lowered to facilitate public participation in the stock market.

Margin call When a stock or commodity declines to the point where it is about to fall below the required margin, the broker demands additional collateral from the investor, failing which his position is sold in the market.

Mark to market Reflecting current market value changes in an appraisal.

Market analysis Great tides flow in the market, and an unemotional investor may be able to improve his odds by taking them into account. In the euphoric times when almost every new issue goes to a premium, and everybody you meet is bullish, the veteran cuts back. In the midst of gloom, when sound values are being jettisoned because they are "going lower," when many companies sell in the market for less than their cash in the bank, and when the subscription services are bearish, he reappears with his bushel basket and sweeps in the bargains.

Of course, euphoria can progress to a manic condition, and gloom degenerate into despair. Nevertheless, it is helpful to know the patient's current status, as measured by odd-lot short sales, mutual fund cash, brokers' credit balances, net advances, and the like. They can be studied in figures or shown in graphic form, like the graphs produced by a lie detector (heartbeat, breathing, sweating, etc.).

This is quite different from the astrology of "double tops" and so forth that the **chartists** (*q.v.*) invoke.

Market capitalization (market cap) The number of shares a company has outstanding times the price per share.

Market return The standard (typically the S&P 500) against which stock portfolio performance can be measured.

Market timing Trying to catch short-term market movements. Extremely difficult.

Market-weighted When an index is based on the market capitalization of the stocks that make it up.

Microcap Refers to companies with a market capitalization in the $100 million to $300 million range.

Midcap Companies with a market capitalization in the $3 billion to $4 billion range.

Modern Portfolio Theory (MPT) A simplistic approach to managing large institutional portfolios. Crudely stated, you decide which way components of the market should go, what degree of volatility and other characteristics you can accept, and then, usually using a computer, choose stocks with those characteristics.

Momentum investing Following the flow of funds in the market, rather than the intrinsic value of the assets purchased. Unfortunately, the river flows fastest just before it crashes over the falls.

Money market The market for fixed-income assets shorter than a year. A money market fund ordinarily holds assets of less than two months' duration.

Morgan Stanley Capital International Europe, Australasian, and Far East Index (MSCI EAFE) A capitalization-weighted dollar index of about one thousand European, Australian, New Zealand, and Far Eastern stocks.

MSCI European Index A capitalization-weighted dollar index of about six hundred European stocks in fourteen countries.

MSCI Pacific Index A capitalization-weighted dollar index of about 350 stocks in Japan, Hong Kong, Singapore, and Malaysia, plus about 70 in Australia and New Zealand.

Multiple Short for price-earnings multiple.

Naked option Usually, a call that is sold when one does not own the underlying stock.

NASDAQ Composite Index Includes all the stocks traded on the NASDAQ, capitalization-weighted.

Negligence Failing to conduct oneself prudently, meaning with care, skill, and caution.

New York Stock Exchange Index Includes all the stocks on the New York Stock Exchange, capitalization-weighted.

Parties of a trust Generally, the person who creates the trust (i.e., the grantor or testator), the trustee, and the beneficiaries.

Passive management Creating a portfolio to match a market index.

Per capita Latin, meaning "by the head." Distributing to "issue per capita" means to distribute trust property to persons who take, in their own right, an equal portion of the property.

Per stirpes Latin, meaning "by the root." Distributing to "issue per stirpes" means to distribute trust property to persons who take, in equal portions, the share which their deceased ancestor would have taken if living.

Perpetuities, Rule Against See **Rule Against Perpetuities**.

Personal trusts Trusts created by and for individuals, as distinguished from business trusts, charitable trusts, employee pension trusts, etc.

Pourover trusts An inter vivos or living trust that receives funds or property interests from a source other than directly from the grantor, usually from the grantor's estate.

Pourover will A will that directs the distribution of part or all of the estate to a preexisting inter vivos trust created by the testator. See **pourover trust**.

Power-in-trust A power, created by statute in some states, that authorizes the holder to keep custody of and manage the interests of a trust or estate vesting in a minor.

Power of appointment A power bestowed upon a beneficiary by a trust grantor or testator to direct the disposition of property in favor of the holder of the power or third parties, exercisable during the holder's life or by the holder's will, as specified in the instrument creating the power of appointment.

Power of attorney A document that designates a legal agent to exercise general or specific financial powers on behalf of the person granting the power.

Power of revocation A power, usually reserved by the grantor of a trust, to revoke it and retake the then corpus.

Power of withdrawal The right in a person to take or remove property (generally principal) from a trust. See also **Crummey power; power of appointment**.

Preferred stock A class of stock with priority rights, both as to dividends and in liquidation, over the common stock of the same company. Corporations pay a much lower income tax on dividends from their investments in other corporations (where it has already been taxed) than on direct business earnings. Preferred stock is usually priced at the level that makes it attractive to a corporation, taking account of this tax exemption, and as a result is rarely tax-efficient for individuals.

Premium The payment for an option.

Presumptive remaindermen Those persons who, if a trust were to terminate at any given time, are entitled to take the then trust corpus.

Price-earnings (P/E) multiple or ratio The number of times its own latest twelve months' earnings that a stock is selling for in the market (e.g., if a stock earns $3 and sells for 30, the P/E is 10).

Principal The corpus or capital of a trust, as distinguished from the income produced.

Private placement A company sells stock to a few investors, usually institutional, without going through the market.

Private trusts A term used to identify trusts created by individuals for individuals, either during life or under will.

Probate The court procedure for proving that an instrument is the last will and testament of a decedent. Testamentary trusts created by a will are not valid until the will is probated.

Profit-taking An absurd euphemism for "selling."

Qualified plan A pension plan funded by a company for its employees, perhaps also with employee contributions. Taxes are paid by the employee upon withdrawal.

Rate of return The internal or discount rate of return of an investment is that interest rate which applied to future earnings reduces them to the present market price.

Real estate investment trust (REIT) A fund that holds real estate assets, whether equity or debt.

Rebalancing If, for instance, a portfolio is supposed to be 50 percent in stocks and 50 percent in fixed income, or 10 percent in emerging markets, or no more than 5 percent in one stock, and price changes throw it out of alignment, to restore the desired allocations you "rebalance." Not as reasonable an idea as it sounds.

Reformation of trust Correcting the terms of a trust, usually with court approval, to eliminate a mistake or ambiguity.

Relative return A portfolio's return compared with its benchmark.

Release To discharge from responsibility and liability.

Remainder The trust corpus existing at the termination of the life beneficiary's interest.

Remaindermen Those who receive the principal at the termination of a trust.

Reserves The fixed-income component of a portfolio, notably shorter-term highly liquid instruments.

Residual risk The **specific risk** contained in a security, as distinct from the general market risk.

Resistance level A price area where a lot of stock has traded in the past which is believed hard to surpass because many investors will want to sell at last.

Restatement of the Law Third, Trusts A book of rules and principles promulgated by the American Law Institute, concerning the conduct of a trustee in the management of a trust. It serves as a guide for lawyers, trustees, and investment advisors.

Return on equity An excellent definition is profit margin × turnover × leverage, where profit margin is sales ÷ profits, turnover is sales ÷ assets, and leverage is assets ÷ equity. It is extremely high in industries with high R&D that is expensed rather than capitalized and added to equity, such as pharmaceuticals.

Revocable trusts Trusts that can be terminated by a power to revoke, usually reserved to the grantor. They do not generally constitute gifts for federal gift tax purposes.

Risk Sometimes confused by theorists with volatility, which in fact offers informed investors a choice. In reality, there exists the inherent risk of a business, or of a country, or of the market (notably the possibility that one is overpaying). Particularly as to bonds, there is also a risk that higher current interest rates will reduce the value of future income.

Risk-free rate of return The ninety-day Treasury bill return. These in fact have some risk, but are nevertheless used as the benchmark.

Rule Against Perpetuities A rule of law that limits the term of trusts to no more than the lives of a reasonable number of persons, named individually or by a class, who are living on the date the trust is created, plus twenty-five years. A trust that violates the rule will terminate earlier as the rule prescribes.

Russell 3000 Index The 3000 largest U.S. companies, capital-weighted, which represent about 98 percent of the investible equity market.

Russell 1000 Index The 1000 largest companies in the Russell 3000 index.

Russell 2000 Index The 2000 smallest companies in the Russell 3000 index.

Safe harbor Practices that satisfy such requirements as the Prudent Investor Rule.

Secondary reaction See **correction**.

Settlor The creator of an inter vivos trust; also same as **grantor, trustor,** or **creator**.

Sharpe ratio Measures return adjusted for risk by subtracting the risk-free return from that achieved by the portfolio and dividing the result by the portfolio's calculated risk level.

Short When you sell a stock that you do not own, hoping to buy it cheaper later on. "Short against the box" means selling short a stock that you do own and expect to keep.

Sideways A stock is somewhat quaintly said to be moving sideways if its price varies little from day to day.

Simple trusts Trusts that direct the payment of all income at least annually to a beneficiary, with no discretion in the trustee to vary the amounts or timing of the payments. See **complex trusts**.

Situs of trust The state of domicile of a trust, determined by such factors as location of assets, residence of trustee, and jurisdiction at inception of trust. It can change.

Size-weighted return (a) Calculating a manager's performance by weighting the size of each account. (b) Of an index (e.g., the S&P 500), weighting each stock by its market capitalization.

Skill One of the three components of the standard of prudence governing trustees; familiarity with business matters.

Small capitalization Companies with market capitalization in the $100 million to $900 million range.

Socially responsible (or targeted) investment Favors socially beneficial and avoids supposedly harmful investments. May be idiosyncratic (e.g., avoiding defense-related or nonunion companies).

Soft dollar Brokerage commissions used to pay for services.

Specific risk See **residual risk**.

Speculating Guessing, by buying an asset that has no underlying earnings, or about whose future price one knows little, such as art or gold.

Spendthrift trust A trust whose beneficiary cannot assign his interest, either under the terms of the trust agreement or under state law.

Split When a stock reaches a high price, the management of the company will split it two for one, three for two, or whatever, to create a lower price per share and thus facilitate trading. The dividend may be raised at the same time.

In a "reverse split," a low-priced stock, often of a failing company, is consolidated to bring the price per share up to a reasonable level. On the Canadian exchanges such stocks are thereafter called "Consolidated Gold Bug" (or whatever).

Split interest trust A trust with both charitable and noncharitable beneficiaries. In addition to the trust agreement and state law, such a trust is also governed by special provisions of the Internal Revenue Code.

Sprinkling trust When the trustee has the discretionary power to pay all, part, or none of trust income or principal, or both, to a single beneficiary or a class of beneficiaries.

Standard and Poor's 500 Composite Stock Index (S&P 500) Four hundred industrial, sixty utility and transportation issues, and forty financials, market-weighted.

Standard deviation For an investment, a measure of the variability from the mean of the return on that investment, and thus a measure of volatility.

Statutory commission Compensation provision for trustees under a specific state statute.

Striking price See **exercising price**.

Strong hands Substantial buyers, whom one presumes will hold for a considerable period. The opposite of **weak hands**.

Supervised trust A trust supervised by a court in certain state jurisdictions.

Surcharge A court-imposed penalty levied against a trustee for committing a breach of trust.

Technical analysis The technical analyst hopes to predict stock movement through **market analysis** or **charting** (*q.v.*), without reference to value. One of the best-known practitioners blacked out his windows to block external distractions.

Testamentary trust A trust created by will.

Title to property The right to ownership of property. In trusts, the trustee has legal title to the trust property, and beneficiaries have beneficial ownership in the property.

Tobin's Q The underlying appraisal value of the corporate assets in a market average, as compared with their market or book value. A useful indicator.

Top-down investment One begins with a theme, such as an attractive industry or country, and then chooses stocks that should participate.

Total return Capital gain plus dividends. See **rate of return**. One version of this expression heard in Wall Street is unsound, namely, the dividend yield from a stock plus the rate at which that yield is growing. For instance, if a stock yields 5 percent, which yield is growing at 15 percent, then the "total return," according to this usage, would be 20 percent. On the other hand, so would a 0.1 percent yield growing at 19.9 percent, which, however, is a much less attractive situation.

Treasury stock A company's own stock repurchased and held for options, purchase of another company, etc.

Trust agreement The document that creates an inter vivos trust, between a grantor and a trustee, for the benefit of the beneficiaries.

Trust indenture A **trust agreement**.

Trust instrument A **trust agreement**.

Trust under deed Created by a trust agreement during the creator's lifetime.

Trust under will A trust created by a will at the time of the testator's death.

Trustor Same as **grantor, donor,** or **settlor**.

"u/a" An abbreviation for "under agreement"; an inter vivos trust (e.g., Trust u/a John Jones, Grantor).

"u/d" An abbreviation for "under deed"; commonly an inter vivos trust. See also **"u/a."**

Up tick A stock trade at a higher price than the last previous transaction.

"u/w" An abbreviation for "under will"; (e.g., Trust u/w John Jones, Testator).

Value investing Buying companies that appear cheap in terms of their underlying assets rather than their long-term growth prospects.

Warrant A right to buy stock, usually attached to a fixed-income security.

Weak hands Speculative retail buyers of stock. See **strong hands**.

Window dressing Toward the end of a reporting period, particularly at year end, mutual funds and banks will sometimes round up their holdings to even thousands, or sell positions that have gone down and thus constitute an eyesore.

Index

About the Authors

JOHN TRAIN received his B.A. and M.A. from Harvard University. After a period in business and then in the Army, he entered the investment advisory profession. He founded his own firm, now Train, Smith Counsel, in 1958. He has written numerous books on investing and other subjects, including *The Money Masters, The New Money Masters* (both translated into many languages), *Preserving Captial and Making It Grow,* and, most recently, *The Craft of Investing.* He has published over 400 pieces as a regular columnist in the *Wall Street Journal, Forbes, Harvard Magazine,* the *Financial Times, Le Matin* (Paris), and elsewhere.

In *Dance of the Money Bees* (1975), he introduced what "is now called swarm theory and modeled in computers . . . Train effectively preceded the entire field of financial economics by over twenty years in using biology as a paradigm" (Christopher T. May, *Nonlinear Pricing: Theory & Applications*).

He is a director of several mutual funds, and has been appointed to part-time positions as a governor or director of independent agencies by Presidents Reagan, Bush, and Clinton.

THOMAS A. MELFE practices trust and estate law as a senior counsel of the law firm of Piper & Marbury L.L.P., New York City.

Prior to 1981, Mr. Melfe was executive vice president and group operating officer of the Trust Services Group of the United States Trust Company of New York. He received his B.A. at Notre Dame University and his law degree at Georgetown Law School. He also served as an officer in the U.S. Marine Corps.

Mr. Melfe has written and lectured extensively on trusts, wills, taxes, and estate planning. He is a fellow of the American College of Trusts and Estate Counsel, and an academician of the International Academy of Estate and Trust Law. He is a fellow of the New York State Bar Foundation, and is chairman of the New York State Bar Association's Investment Committee.

Mr. Melfe has served as chairman of the board of the Municipal Fund for New York Investors, Inc., sponsored by PNC Institutional Management Corporation, and as a director of the family of twenty-four mutual funds sponsored by Warburg, Pincus & Co.